Using P
on Boa

Other titles of interest

Using GPS   Conrad Dixon   ISBN 0-7136-4738-8

Using GPS aims to help owners get the best from their sets and make full use of the facilities available, whether simply position fixing and course setting or interfacing with integrated navigation systems. Seven current sets are compared function by function.

GMDSS: A User's Handbook   Denise Bréhaut   ISBN 0-7136-4837-6

Anyone with GMDSS equipment on board their boat will need an operator's licence. This book has been written to alleviate the fears and confusion surrounding GMDSS. It explains the operation of the system as a whole and the procedures involved, as well as covering the syllabi of the various operators' certificates.

Understanding Weatherfax   Mike Harris   ISBN 0-7136-4344-7

How do you turn the symbols on the weather chart into a meaningful forecast? Armed with this book and a current weatherfax chart you will have all the essentials for making your own forecast no matter where you are in the world.

Waypoint Directory   Peter Cumberlidge   ISBN 0-7136-4117-7

An invaluable reference for anyone navigating with GPS whether under sail or power. It contains 60 coastal approach charts for the English and French sides of the English Channel, showing the positions and details of over 500 carefully chosen waypoints. Alongside each clear waypoint chart is a table giving the latitude and longitude of each waypoint, as well as details of the coastal dangers.

North Sea Waypoint Directory   Peter Cumberlidge   ISBN 0-7136-4799-X

Following the highly successful *English Channel Waypoints Directory*, the *North Sea Waypoint Directory* will be welcomed by anyone planning a passage in the southern North Sea. It contains 67 approach and landfall charts with over 800 waypoints from Dover Strait to the Humber and from Calais to Esbjerg.

Using PCs on Board

Rob Buttress & Tim Thornton

ADLARD COLES NAUTICAL
London

Published 2000 by Adlard Coles Nautical
an imprint of A & C Black (Publishers) Ltd
35 Bedford Row, London WC1R 4JH

ISBN 0-7136-5289-6

A CIP catalogue record for this book is available from the British Library.

Typeset in Optimum 10/12

Printed and bound in Great Britain by
The Cromwell Press, Trowbridge, Wiltshire.

Contents

Acknowledgements

The authors are grateful for permission to use the following photographs and illustrations:

Bonito – Page 66, 68
Bernard Clack – 109
Dartcom – Page 72 (top)
Euronav Ltd – Front cover, page 35, 39, 111
Icom (UK) Ltd – Front cover, back cover, 56
ICS Electronics Ltd – Front cover, page 71, 72 (bottom)
Lightmaster Software – Page 79 (both)
Maptech Inc – Page 30, 40
Maritek – 138
Merlin Equipment – Page 118 (both)
Marine Computing International Ltd – Page 45, 46, 51, 52, 61,
        77, 81, 93, 95, 108
Nautical Data Ltd – Page 49, 50, 78
Nautical Publications – Front cover, page 30
Neptune Software – Page 48
Next O'Gara – Back cover, page 26, 60, 64
Noonmark Yachting – Front cover, page 111
David Parrott – 24, 102, 103, 104 (both)
PC Maritime Ltd – Page 17, 33, 65, 80
SCS Elettronica – Page 38, 41, 42
Techman – Page 74
Trimble Navigation Europe Ltd – Page 62

In addition, the authors would like to thank James Hortop of Merlin Equipment for advice on inverters and power supplies; Dr David Lovering of Optima Research and Nichola Woodward for painstaking proofreading.

Electronic chart images reproduced courtesy of the Controller of Her Majesty's Stationery Office United Kingdom Hydrographic Office and others. Marine software systems including electronic charting systems are not a replacement for traditional navigational methods and should be used prudently. Chart images included in this book are not for navigation.

All trademarks are acknowledged as being the property of their respective owners.

Who is this book for?

This book is intended for the large and growing number of yachtsmen and women who are contemplating using a personal computer on board their (or someone else's) yacht or motorboat. You may already have a laptop computer and want to know what it can do for you, or wish to extend its capabilities, or you may be thinking of buying a computer as an alternative to expensive, dedicated instruments.

Whatever the case, there is such a vast array of conflicting information available that even when you *have* made a choice, there's often a nagging doubt that you have made the wrong one. Hopefully this book will make your choice easier, reassure you that you have made the right decision, or at least show you where you have gone wrong so that you can get it right next time!

This book is **not** written for computer buffs or enthusiasts. It is written for ordinary cruising and racing sailors and powerboaters, starting at the most basic level and using everyday terms. It also includes a glossary to help explain some of the marketing and technical phrases that you will inevitably encounter. If you are generally familiar with computers, you should still find this book useful because it is not an everyday computer manual, but instead attempts to explain the technology in a way that is relevant to boat users.

In the fast moving computer world, it is likely that some of the technologies in use and terminology will change over the life of this book. To help keep the information current, the authors maintain a World Wide Web site on the Internet with up-to-date information and links to equipment manufacturers' and other sites of interest. The web site address is http://www.pconboard.co.uk (if you don't understand this or want to learn more about the Internet, turn to chapter 8). Generally speaking, 'currently' means the late 1990s and 'the future' means the first few years of the new millennium.

Finally, PC doesn't just stand for 'personal computer'! In the interests of being 'politically correct' and not offending anyone, we have tried to use terms that are not gender-specific. We could not quite bring ourselves to use that bland PC term 'boater', so where we refer to 'yachtsman/men' etc, we mean all sailors, whatever their sex. Similarly, the term 'yachtsman' refers to those of you who take pleasure from using any reasonably sized boat on the water, whether propelled primarily by sails, or by a motor.

About the Authors

Rob Buttress has sailed for over twenty years. After completing his studies he joined the computer industry to learn the ropes from the ground up, working on programming, hardware and sales and marketing projects.

More recently, Rob has sailed the Atlantic circuit, encountering many sailors who knew they needed a PC, but didn't know what to buy or how to make it work for them. Currently, Rob is marketing manager of a leading navigational software and data publisher and a marine electronic systems consultant. He is also a member of the Royal Institute of Navigation.

Tim Thornton studied naval architecture, and worked on yacht design and race handicapping systems. After taking a degree in maths and computing, he became a marine computing research scientist for IBM as well as one of the pioneers in on board computer systems for racing yachts.

Tim now runs a company specialising in on board marine computing systems. His experience ranges from supplying systems to offshore racers in events such as the *Around Alone* and *Volvo Round the World Races* through to superyachts, as well as providing for the needs of the normal weekend sailor or club racer.

He is the author of *'The Offshore Yacht'* and *'The Small Offshore Yacht'*.

Why bother, why now?

Throughout the late 1980s and early 1990s, there *were* yachtsmen who were brave, rich or enthusiastic enough to take computers on board their yachts or motorboats. Often, the computers cost as much as a small family car and the programs they used were relatively amateurish and fairly unreliable. Couple this with sometimes poor and underpowered on board electrical installations and you wonder why they ever bothered in the first place!

The reason is that yachtsmen quickly found such systems really aided their sailing, giving accurate, timely information and taking a lot of the slog out of navigational calculations. For cruisers, this allowed them to spend more time actually enjoying the sailing; and racers became much more competitive because they had tools to identify performance trends both as they happened, and after the race, and to analyse their boat and crew's performance better than ever before.

Generally speaking, though, the systems used were slow, fairly unreliable and very expensive, so the technology was indeed confined to the wealthy and the enthusiastic. As so often happens, it is developments outside the marine leisure field that have brought benefits to the yachtsman. The massive explosion in PC sales caused by such things as the Internet and multimedia has really brought prices down and we are now at a stage where the use of PCs on board leisure boats is extremely common, especially in the 9 metre (27 feet) plus, range.

But it's not only because PCs have become genuinely affordable – they have also become much more reliable and powerful; and the software running on them has become far, far better than was the case even a very few years ago.

Often with computers, people would rather 'wait and see' before committing to a purchase, in the hope that something better comes along soon at a lower price. The message of this book is **don't** – good, affordable and reliable systems are here **now**, and to wait would deny you the many benefits to be had from using them. Additionally, where some older programs were designed to lock you into particular (often proprietary) technologies, nowadays they are often designed to be 'open', allowing you choice and flexibility, and a lower-cost upgrade path for the future.

There has never been a better time to get started. So, if you could do with an extra crew member to help you with tidal calculations, route planning, plotting and logging, performance analysis, receiving weather information, communications, even astro sight reductions, read on.

Size *is* important...

There are obviously some vessels that are simply too small or 'too wet' to have a computer on board. There is typically a minimum size of boat that might use a PC on board – a couple of years ago, that might have been 15 metres LOA (45 feet), but nowadays it's common to see boats as small as 8½ metres LOA (25 feet), some even less, with PCs on board.

Even if you have a 5½ metre (16 feet), half-decked fishing boat, you may still be able to use the power of a PC – to work out the tides, for example, or to plan fishing trips – but this would be done at home, not on the boat. You can 'download' waypoints from electronic charting systems into a hand-held GPS, or print out the tides for the day onto paper, seal it into a polythene pocket and take that with you.

So how small is too small? This is a difficult question to answer, and will be a commonsense decision that you make for yourself, based on the size and general characteristics of your boat as well as the depth of your pocket. To help you to decide, speak to other people – marinas and yacht club bars are great places to pick other people's brains for information.

What do you need?

The most basic set-up, and certainly the most common, is a laptop PC, powered directly by the boat's battery supply or through a small inverter, probably connected to a hand-held GPS (Global Positioning System) set, and with basic software loaded. Even this simple set-up is extremely powerful. This could be used for simple chart plotting and calculation-based tasks such as working out the state of the tide at a given time or reducing sextant observations for position lines. Word processing software lets you keep a narrative log, or details stores loaded below; with other familiar

A simple set-up: a laptop PC connected to a GPS set and running chart plotting software

'office-type' software, for example a spreadsheet, you could keep the boat's accounts; in harbour, multimedia CD-ROMs and computer games can keep the children (and adults) amused.

This kind of set-up can be bought very inexpensively, certainly for less than the cost of a colour 'chart plotter' or a couple of navigation instrument repeater heads. It doesn't stop there though: the wonderful thing about using a PC is that it's remarkably cheap to add features; for a little extra, you can have a fully featured and very sophisticated system, without having to trade in your PC each time you want to add a function.

What else can you do with it?

On top of the basic set-up described above, it's simple to connect a PC to the following equipment:

◆ **Other electronic navigation instruments** (log, depth, wind, compass, etc) – This can allow you to display *and keep a log* of data provided by your instruments – great for convenience and performance analysis.

◆ **Radar** – Although it would not be a good idea to obscure valuable chart data with a scanned radar image, several chart plotting systems can show moving vessel targets on top of the electronic chart, and export a 'marker flag', representing a known point on the chart, to the radar. Systems are now appearing where the PC plotting software directly controls a radar and the scanned radar image is skilfully blended with the chart image so as not to obscure chart information.

◆ **Autopilot** – Using chart plotting software you can quickly plan and re-plan routes, and some systems even take the tide into account – imagine being able to feed a realistic course to steer to your autopilot after every waypoint change.

◆ **Single Side Band (SSB) receiver** – Connect your PC to the audio output of your SSB to receive detailed weather maps; receive Morse code, radio-telex and NAVTEX using the same connection, all free of charge. With an SSB transceiver and a suitable modem, you can even send radio-telex and e-mail messages.

◆ **Satcom** – Connect to an INMARSAT C unit for global e-mail, or use the growing number of satellite communications services to send and receive faxes or even surf the World Wide Web.

◆ **Mobile phone** – Send and receive faxes or download information from the Internet at low cost via a GSM data card plugged into your mobile telephone.

◆ **Printer** – Though not essential, a printer on board really helps, whether it be to produce hard-copy of weatherfaxes, a back-up printed copy of the log, or pilotage information to use (in a polypocket) in the cockpit when approaching an unfamiliar landfall.

If you already own or use a PC, maybe at home or at work, you'll be aware of some of the possibilities. But for all of you who would like to take a PC on board, the following chapters will guide you through the choices you'll need to make to have a powerful, useful system.

1 • The PC: Hardware, Software and Data

What is a PC?

Many people use PC as a general term when referring to many different kinds of personal computers. However, a widely accepted definition (which we adopted for the purposes of this book) is:

'An IBM compatible computer, running MS-DOS or Microsoft Windows operating systems, and probably equipped with an RS232 serial port and a parallel printer port.'

Though a bit of a mouthful, this definition is important because there are other types of personal computer that, for the sake of brevity, are not covered in detail in this book. Though different types of personal computer may have a place on your vessel, the above definition will, in the authors' opinion, give you the greatest possible choice in terms of the uses to which you may put the system. It should also allow you to easily and cost-effectively keep your system up-to-date. See *Appendix 1 – Other Types of Personal Computer,* for a brief description of alternative computers that you may consider using on board.

What's in the box?

There are three basic elements to any PC system that you might use on board. Described in more detail later on, briefly they are:

Hardware – the physical components that make up the PC: screen, keyboard, mouse, disk drives etc. Usually, your PC also has an 'operating system' (or 'system software') installed when you buy it; this special software provides you with an easy and consistent way of controlling the PC. See chapter 9, Choosing a PC System, for an in-depth discussion of the various parts of a PC and advice on how to interpret manufacturers' specifications.

Application software – so called to distinguish it from the operating system, this is usually called just 'software' or a 'program'.

Being able to run application software is why you bought your PC in the first place, and provides you with the tools to do a particular job. For example, you might buy a program to work out tide times, a full electronic-charting system, or software to write letters (a word processor). You can buy as many different programs for your PC as you like so long as they will work with your operating system and so long as the PC is powerful enough to run them. Unless you purchase your PC from a marine computing specialist, it is unlikely that it will be supplied with marine application software.

Chapters 2 to 8 explain various types of application software that you might use on board, and chapter 9 advises you on choosing a PC that is suitable for the program(s) you want to use.

Data – whatever software you have purchased, it will need data to work with. Data is really a computer word for 'information', and is something you supply yourself (eg typing a letter in a word processor) or purchase (eg electronic charts or tidal information).

Some application software will include at least some of the data it needs; for example, it may have tide-table information included.

Tip – Useful data usually belongs to someone and may be copyrighted because it is very expensive to provide. Thus watch out for software that uses time-limited data or that has data in it for a particular geographical area – the chances are that you will need to buy updates or enhanced coverage. This is not usually unreasonable, but always ask if the software will allow you to add data yourself should you not wish to buy updates.

What else is required?

It is usual that when you purchase a PC, it is supplied with all the hardware required. It will probably also have an operating system (usually Microsoft Windows 98) installed. Many home PC suppliers are also in the habit of including what they term 'bundles' of application software, already installed on the PC's hard disk. Often, 'bundled' software is of limited use on board and, if not pre-installed, should be left in the box, unless you believe you have a use for it.

To have a useful system on board, you will need to purchase application software and data. You may also need to buy an 'inverter', to power it from your boat's 12V or 24V batteries; and an 'interface' cable, to connect the PC to on board instrument(s) such as a GPS set. These issues are described in more detail in chapter 10, Installing your PC.

The tools: software and data

One of the great things about PCs is that they can be used for virtually anything that involves the processing of words or numbers. That said, there are occasions when 'doing it by computer' is just not worth the effort – sometimes good old pen and paper, or even the humble human brain, is the best solution. These areas include things associated with human judgement and experience, or where source data isn't currently available or accurate enough.

With suitable software, PCs can be useful for many different tasks on board, especially if connected to external equipment

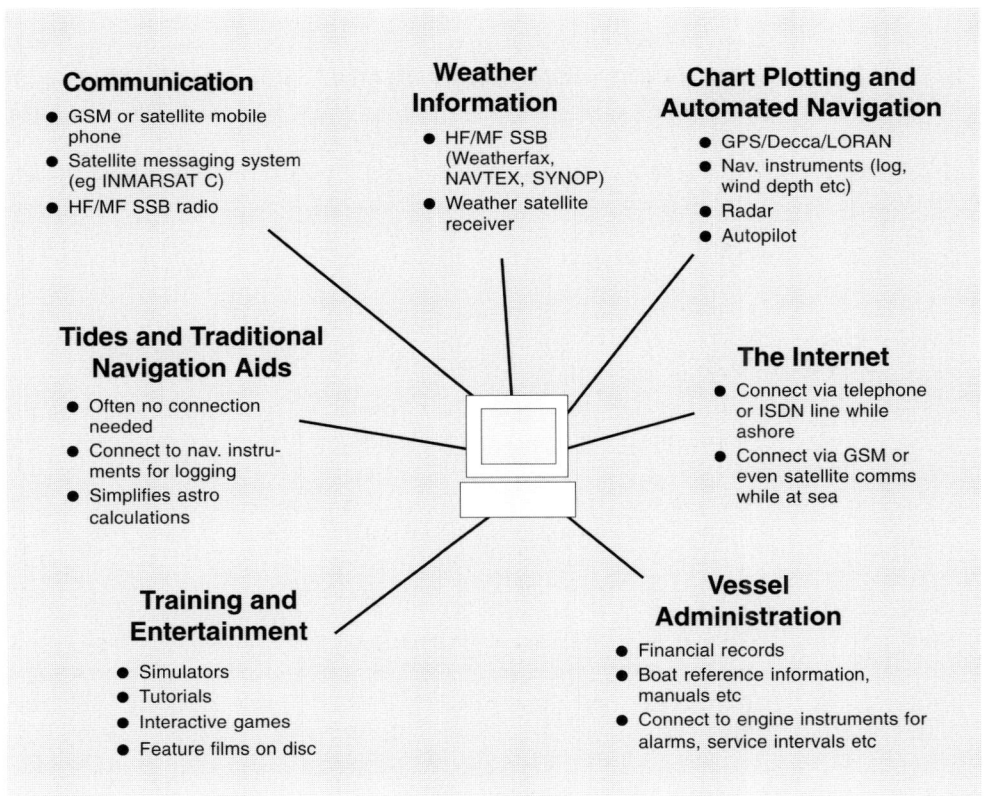

Nevertheless, whilst PCs can't grind winches, they are particularly adept at handling repetitive calculations accurately and at processing raw data and presenting it as 'real information' so that the user can make decisions based on it.

There are many areas of leisure boating where the power of PCs will help you enjoy your sport more, or even become better at it.

Communication
- GSM or satellite mobile phone
- Satellite messaging system (eg INMARSAT C)
- HF/MF SSB radio

Weather Information
- HF/MF SSB (Weatherfax, NAVTEX, SYNOP)
- Weather satellite receiver

Chart Plotting and Automated Navigation
- GPS/Decca/LORAN
- Nav. instruments (log, wind depth etc)
- Radar
- Autopilot

Tides and Traditional Navigation Aids
- Often no connection needed
- Connect to nav. instruments for logging
- Simplifies astro calculations

The Internet
- Connect via telephone or ISDN line while ashore
- Connect via GSM or even satellite comms while at sea

Training and Entertainment
- Simulators
- Tutorials
- Interactive games
- Feature films on disc

Vessel Administration
- Financial records
- Boat reference information, manuals etc
- Connect to engine instruments for alarms, service intervals etc

These applications can be broadly split into the six areas shown below, which are described in detail in the following chapters:

2   Chart Plotting and Automated Navigation
3   Tides and Traditional Navigation Aids
4   Communications
5   Weather Information
6   Vessel Administration
7   Training and Entertainment

Additionally, we will take a short look at the Internet in chapter 8. Although it's not likely that the average yachtsman will currently be 'surfing the Internet' from on board, this will undoubtedly happen in time; most importantly, though, there are a large number of resources available on the Internet which are of use to yachtsmen.

The following chapters explore the six main types of marine software available. Where possible, the authors have avoided the use of trade or brand names, and readers should be aware that unless stated clearly as fact, statements made are solely the opinion of the authors.

2 • Chart Plotting and Automated Navigation

Chart plotting, or electronic charting, is probably the biggest single reason for purchasing a PC for use on board. Most yachtsmen have a Global Positioning System (GPS) set and the addition of a PC and suitable software can give you an automatic chart plotting capability very similar to that used on board the largest merchant and naval vessels.

If you already own a suitable computer, then using PC-based electronic charting software provides an extremely low cost solution – usually far less than purchasing a dedicated colour chart plotter – whilst giving access to the highest quality navigational charts and very powerful navigation functions.

Note that as well as GPS receivers, most electronic charting systems will work with Loran and differential GPS (DGPS), even Decca sets, as long as they can export latitude and longitude information in a suitable format.

Even a simple laptop-based set-up can be very powerful. Here PC Maritime's Navmaster is interfaced to on board instruments

Choosing an electronic charting system

There is now a large choice of electronic charting software available and it can be tempting to rush into the process of choosing a system on the basis of one or two appealing features seen at a boat show presentation. Do bear in mind that some features are so important that they should be considered before all others. For example, even if a particular product has all the bells and whistles that you think you need, if it won't run on your type of computer, or does not have the chart coverage for the areas you sail in, it is obviously not worth considering.

One of the really important questions that should be addressed first is *chart compatibility*. Some chart plotting systems will only work with one brand of electronic chart, so if you have identified a system to purchase, check very carefully that charts are available for the area you are interested in, and that you are satisfied with the quality and detail of those charts.

Choosing a system therefore could perhaps be regarded as a back-to-front process, with the actual system features being compared after deciding which kind of electronic charts you wish to use. For this reason, we'll look at electronic charts first before investigating what electronic charting systems have to offer.

Choosing electronic charts

There are two main kinds of technology used in the manufacture of electronic charts; these are concerned with how the chart data itself is actually stored in the electronic chart. The two technologies are called raster and vector, and give each type of chart particular characteristics, which are discussed in the section below.

Raster charts

Nearly all raster charts are produced by feeding an original complete paper chart (or the printing films that were used to produce it) through a large-format digital scanner. This converts the chart information into a computer file comprised of a grid (a raster) of dots (or pixels) of varying colour. The resulting computer file is then geo-referenced so it may be used with electronic charting software. Geo-referencing is simply providing information so that a real-world latitude and longitude position can be automatically converted to a position on the chart, and vice versa, allowing for any differences between the GPS and chart datum. Following geo-referencing, raster charts undergo a final quality assurance process and are then stored as computer files in a special format to help them load into the PC as quickly as possible. Often, the raster chart files will also be encrypted so that they may only be used with certain electronic charting systems.

The chart is scanned at sufficiently high resolution, anything up to 250 dots per inch (dpi), so that in normal use, the user's eyes are fooled into seeing the complete chart image rather than the dots that comprise it. The drawback with scanning the chart at a very high resolution is that the chart files are large and take a long time to draw – a laptop PC screen has a resolution of about 70dpi.

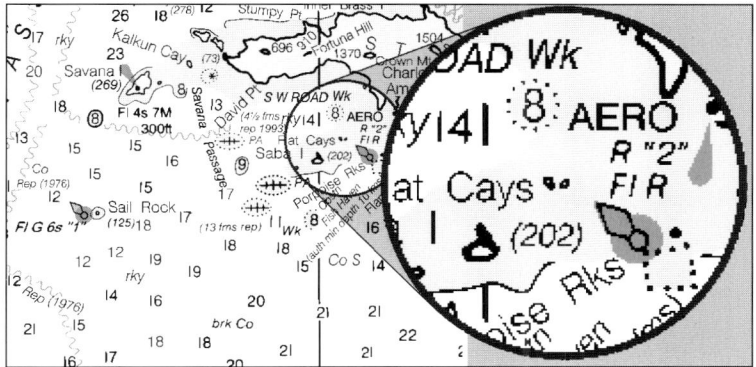

Like a newspaper photograph, a raster chart is comprised of a pattern of dots

Raster charts have the benefit that they appear on-screen exactly the same as the original paper version, and therefore navigators tend to have a high degree of confidence in them. They are also relatively quicker and cheaper to produce than vector charts, thus worldwide coverage is significant and growing fast. A drawback is that the chart files are quite large, and that although they may look good when viewed at their 'scanned-in' scale, when you zoom out to see more of the chart on the screen the quality of the image can deteriorate markedly. If the software you are using permits you to zoom in to the chart to any great extent, you will soon start to see the dots that comprise it.

Vector charts

The technology used to create vector charts is more advanced than that used for raster charts. In a vector chart, each chart feature is stored as a mathematical vector describing its shape and size, rather than as a pattern of dots. They can be created in several different ways.

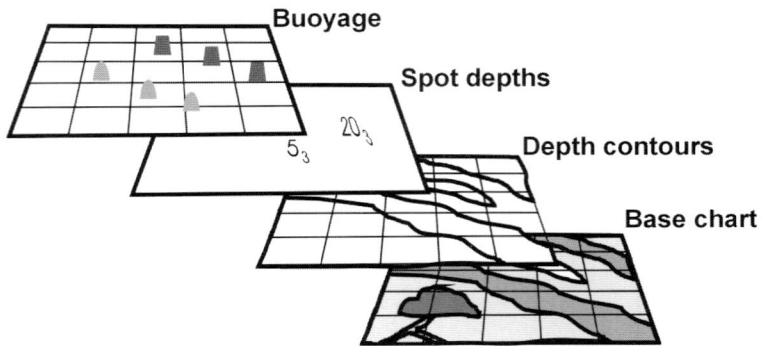

Buoyage

Spot depths

Depth contours

Base chart

Vector charts are actually made up of a series of layers

Firstly, they may be created by fixing a paper chart onto a 'digitising tablet'; this is a flat table which has a grid of electronic wires embedded in it. An operator moves an electronic 'puck' or cursor over the features on the chart, and the location of the puck is recorded by the network of wires. In this way, the location of every feature on the chart is translated by the digitising software into a vector database of the chart features.

Nowadays, very few vector charts are created using this old-fashioned method, which is quite slow and limited in accuracy. Many charts are now created using a 'head-up' digitising process. With head-up digitising, the paper or film original is scanned in much the same way as for a raster chart; the resulting raster computer file is then displayed on a PC screen, and an operator traces each chart feature using a pointer on-screen. This method is far more accurate than using a digitising tablet; it is also much faster, because the digitising software can perform specialised tasks such as semi-automatic line following.

Because experienced humans carry out both of these methods, it is possible to not only record the location of each feature, but also to group similar features together, or to include 'attributes' that further define each feature. Similar types of features may be stored on 'layers' and, by doing this, the chart can be said to include some form of 'intelligence'. For example, an electronic chart system could interrogate the vector chart to find the value of the nearest spot depth, or to provide further information on a navigational mark.

Currently, the vast majority of vector charts are created as described above. But already, the new generation of official vector charts are being produced by a combination of head-up digitising and 'direct data import'. Direct data import has become possible as an increasing amount of hydrographic survey data is captured and stored electronically – an electronic chart may now be produced completely electronically, with no paper being involved at all.

Hybrid charts

There is another kind of electronic chart, which we will probably see more of in the years to come, and that is the hybrid chart. Most electronic charting professionals recognise that both raster and vector technologies have their strengths. The hybrid chart is an attempt to offer the best of both worlds, by combining 'intelligent' vector data with a raster backdrop. Although it is too early to say whether these kinds of charts will be important in the future, the technology does look promising and they are already used in some land mapping packages, such as Microsoft's *Autoroute*.

So which is better, raster or vector?

This is a very common question from those who are new to electronic charting. The straight answer is that neither raster nor vector is inherently better than the other type.

Certainly, raster charts include none of the intelligence of vector charts, they are a simple, flat picture and for this reason vector charts are often seen as being superior to raster. It is true to say that for some particular specialist applications, the extra functionality of vector chart may win out over raster, however, for general purpose small craft navigation, the choice comes down largely to personal preference.

For this reason, the reader who wishes to purchase an electronic charting system is advised to choose a system that lets them use both types as standard. If not, they should satisfy themselves as to which kind of electronic charts they prefer before making a purchase, as it is seldom possible to return electronic charts on the basis of preference.

In conclusion, raster charts are familiar to the navigator because they appear identical to the paper charts from which they were scanned. They are also simple to use and no special knowledge or training is required to use them safely and effectively. Vector charts on the other hand are intelligent in that chart layers can be 'interrogated' by charting software eg querying depth contours. Also, their relatively small file size means they tend to display quickly and can give a clearer display than raster charts by allowing features to be shown sharply for each zoom level.

Chart manufacturers

There is intense competition between the manufacturers of the various kinds of electronic charts currently available. This is not surprising because there is a lot of money to be made out of electronic charts in the years ahead. This is mainly from the commercial sector, so it's no surprise that it is their requirements, rather than those of leisure yachtsmen, that tend to be taken into account.

To show there's no preference from the authors, the companies are listed in strictly alphabetical order!

◆ **C-Map** (NT and ECDIS standards)
C-Map is probably the oldest existing manufacturer of vector charts. This Italian company has a sizeable collection of charts in a variety of formats. Historically most of its charts were used on dedicated plotters; however, a large and growing number of PC-based systems use C-Map charts. One of the reasons for this is the introduction of the new C-Map NT format, which offers significant detail improvements over previous formats as well as excellent worldwide coverage

◆ **Euronav** (Livechart 'B')
These charts are digitised in England from paper charts and also created from digital data imported from hydrographic offices. The charts are sold either as single charts by chart number, or grouped into special value packs offering area coverage at a reduced cost. Coverage is best in Europe, the Mediterranean and the Caribbean. Commercial update contracts are available.

◆ **Maptech** (ChartPacks, ChartKits, PhotoCharts)
This American chart manufacturer has a long history of producing raster charts, originally as Resolution Mapping. Maptech is the official producer of NOAA charts for the US government. It produces charts in the ChartKit (AKA BSB), ChartPack and PhotoChart formats. Initially coverage was US-centric, but Maptech has recently launched a range of European charts (in the ChartPack format) based on British Admiralty paper charts. Coverage is also good in the Caribbean and the Mediterranean. The PhotoCharts are actually satellite photos, geo-referenced so as to display on screen like charts.

◆ **Mapmedia**
These raster charts are made by the French company Informatique et Mer for use with its MaxSea system.

- **Navionics**
  Like C-Map, Navionics is one of the older vector chart producers. Until recently, almost all of its output was in cartridge form for dedicated plotters, but now a few PC systems work with its 'Floppy Charts'.
- **Softchart**
  A US company producing raster charts with international coverage, though best coverage is to be found in US waters.
- **Transas/Passport**
  Transas offers a large worldwide catalogue of detailed vector charts. Originally, much of its catalogue was based on Russian cartography; more recently, however, a greater proportion of its charts is based on UK Hydrographic Office paper charts. For smaller craft, Transas charts are available under the Passport brand.
- **UK Hydrographic Office** (ARCS)
  The Admiralty Raster Charting Service (ARCS) offers most of the British Admiralty's range of paper charts in its own raster format. There are two levels of service, Navigator (a weekly updated service aimed at commercial users) and Skipper, aimed at the leisure user (where updates can be purchased as frequently as weekly). All available charts are supplied on eleven 'area CDs' and can be unlocked from the CD when required by obtaining a code from the UK Hydrographic Office. Other hydrographic offices (Australia, New Zealand and the Republic of South Africa) are producing charts in a format similar to ARCS.

Other electronic chart issues

Copyright

Carrying out accurate surveys of the seabed and preparing navigational charts is an incredibly expensive business, typically performed by governments rather than private organisations. Because of the high cost of production, chart manufacturers are understandably concerned about mariners making illegal copies of paper charts and are rigorous in enforcing copyright.

Although in certain parts of the world the practice of photocopying paper charts is quite widespread, providing chart data electronically makes it much more susceptible to illegal copying. For this reason, some producers of electronic charts employ some form of hardware copy protection to prevent illegal copying (see dongles, overleaf). One notable exception is for chart data produced by some American companies – many American electronic charts are royalty free and are freely copyable – though they are priced at such a low level that users prefer to buy rather than steal them.

Dongles

A 'dongle', or 'security key', is a small hardware device which is used by software manufacturers to prevent illegal copying of software and data. It is characterised by having a unique number and normally consists of a small amount of electronic circuitry and some memory. The whole lot is encased in plastic and fitted with a connector at one end that fits the PC and usually another connector to which a peripheral such as a printer may be connected.

At the most basic level, the software manufacturer designs his program so that while it is running, it periodically checks that a valid dongle is present. If not, the program will shut down.

More sophisticated dongles will have enough memory fitted so that the software manufacturer can store data in it – this may include 'permissions' to allow certain features of the software to operate, or permissions allowing particular electronic charts to be used. In this way, even if an unscrupulous user makes an illegal copy of a program or data, since they can't replicate the dongle, they won't be able to use the stolen software or data.

Dongles are a very effective method of copy protection and are almost universally used by European electronic charting system manufacturers; however, yachtsmen feel vulnerable that if the dongle fails whilst at sea, they will not be able to use their program and charts. In fact, dongles are solid-state devices and, if treated with reasonable care, are extremely reliable; indeed some designs may last almost indefinitely. It is worth pointing out, though, that since the dongle effectively represents the entire value of the

Some software packages will not run unless their dongle is plugged into the PC

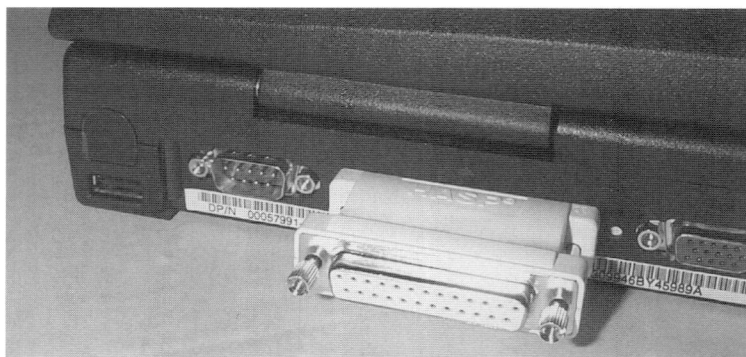

product and data that require its presence, you should take care of it and insure it against all risks, just as you would with the PC you have it plugged into.

Manufacturers will almost certainly refuse to replace lost or stolen dongles, but may at their discretion, and for a fee, replace dongles returned to them which have been damaged by fire or water etc. Note the use of the phrase 'at their discretion' and do not be tempted to open the case of the dongle since any suggestion of tampering will normally prevent the manufacturer from replacing a dongle.

Many dongles are designed to fit into the PC's parallel (printer) port, though there are some serial port dongles and new ones are becoming available that work via PC Card or USB technology. USB dongles look very promising for electronic charting systems because they may also be used to connect the PC to navigation instruments etc.

Although they generally work very well, there are some problems associated with using dongles.

◆ Firstly, to function they require electrical power that they draw from the connector they are plugged into. Some users with very recent notebook computers have reported dongle problems, and it is suspected that in the quest for longer battery lives, some laptops fail to deliver sufficient electrical power to the dongle. If you experience this, it may be worth switching off any power-saving features on the PC.

◆ The dongle is usually connected directly to the printer port on the PC and secured by tightening the supplied screws. Although it is not usually a problem with desktop or Marine PCs, on laptops the dongle normally sticks out from the back of the PC and can be vulnerable to damage. A solution to this is to purchase a small extension, consisting of male and female 25-pin connectors and a short length of flexible ribbon cable. In this way, the dongle could be taped to the back of the lid of the laptop, whilst still being electrically connected to the printer port.

◆ Some modern printers come with 'anti-social' driver software that can affect the operation of the dongle. If this occurs, your only real choices are to disable the printer driver when using the program that requires the dongle or, if possible, to add a second printer port.

Which navigator?

Although some yachtsmen have quite sophisticated systems, with many different navigational instruments interfaced together, the most common set-up is to have just a GPS (or DGPS or Loran) receiver connected to the PC.

You might assume it is possible to interface all navigators to a computer, but in fact not all are capable of this. Many of the cheapest hand-held units are simply unable to export data at all, while some of those that can are unable to do so unless connected to the boat's DC electrical supply by an optional cable.

In order to work with a PC, the navigator must be able to export data in the NMEA0183 format, so if you are planning to purchase a GPS set to use with a PC, you should check this out. Also, some owners of 'networked' or 'integrated' instrument systems may discover that it is impossible to get instrument data onto the PC unless they purchase an external interface box which converts the manufacturer's own data language into NMEA0183 (see page 122).

While shopping around for a GPS set, remember that many PC based electronic charting systems are able to 'upload' lists of waypoints or routes to a suitable navigator. This can be a very useful function, but check the GPS specifications carefully – not all units that export data can also import it.

If you are planning to use your existing navigator, you can check the instruction manual to find out if it can export and import NMEA0183 data – if this doesn't tell you, contact the company you bought it from or contact the manufacturer direct for advice.

Hand-held or fixed GPS sets are suitable, but check they 'speak' NMEA0183

Are paper charts still required?

The legal position is quite clear for large commercial vessels and, although it is less so for leisure vessels, it is important to note that electronic charts are not legal replacements for paper charts. Navigators should always carry up-to-date official charts, and consult them frequently.

Irrespective of the legal situation, it is undoubtedly poor seamanship to rely on just one means of position fixing, whatever it is, and it makes obvious commonsense to have a non-electronic back-up in case of power or equipment failure on board.

Many small craft navigators compromise, by using a PC-based electronic charting system as their primary navigation system, with a smaller number of smaller-scale paper charts as a back-up.

Chart datums

All of us who are used to navigating in tidal waters will be familiar with the term 'chart datum' – this term is often used to describe the depth of water over chart features at (usually) the Lowest Astronomical Tide (LAT), and Highest Astronomical Tide (HAT) for air gaps, in Europe. By taking the height of tide from local tide tables, and adding it to the charted depth over datum, we can quickly get an idea of how much water there actually is at a given point.

This 'chart datum' is actually the 'vertical datum', a reference or starting point from which heights and depths of various chart features are measured. It is not a geographically fixed datum, but rather varies locally – for example, as you sail up-river the vertical datum is moved up to match the rising river bed.

With GPS navigation and electronic charting, the navigator is also very concerned with horizontal datums. A horizontal datum is a model of the shape of the earth in the area covered by the chart, primarily concerned with the diameter of the earth and how far off spherical it is. Some datums such as WGS84 are global, whilst others are regional, for example the OSGB36 datum used round UK waters.

The use of the WGS84 datum is an essential part of the Global Positioning System, and all GPS receivers calculate their position in this datum. However, most paper charts (and therefore electronic charts) are referenced to datums other than WGS84, thus when plotting a position directly from a GPS set (that has been set to display WGS84) onto a non WGS84 paper chart, the position will probably be wrong. Around the UK, where the Ordnance Survey of Great Britain 1936 (OSGB36) or European Datum 1950 (ED50) datums are commonly used, the position error is generally less than 200 metres, but in some parts of the world errors of up to three miles have been reported.

In practice, the situation isn't as bad as it sounds, since for most of the common marine chart datums, fairly accurate offsets from WGS84 are known, or can be automatically worked out using polynomial calculations. These corrections may reduce the error to a few metres (depending upon the scale of the chart in question).

An electronic charting system may give the user the ability to apply these datum corrections automatically, not at all, or to use user-supplied corrections. With good-quality charts, where the position shift to the WGS84 datum is known accurately, the best option is to leave the GPS set outputting WGS84, and have the chart plotter correct this to the chart datum. This is because the processors in GPS receivers do not always have the computing space and power for accurate conversion between different datums.

> **Important Note** – Before GPS navigation became common, few navigators were aware of, or needed to know about, horizontal chart datums, because their navigation (at least in sight of land) tended to be *relative* to visible chart features. With the advent of *absolute* navigation, using highly accurate satellite-derived positions, small craft navigators should be aware that the charts (whether paper or electronic) they are using may not be as accurate as their position-fixing equipment. Therefore they should build in a suitable safety margin when planning passages or navigating. ***This is particularly the case with the much higher precision available with differential GPS (DGPS) receivers.***

Depth units

While the whole world is now officially 'metricated', many paper charts are still in print which are based on surveys carried out decades ago. Electronic charts taken from these paper charts will almost certainly use either feet or fathoms/feet as their depth units. Although new editions of these charts are usually metric, it will be some years before all charts are published using metric depths. **For this reason, the electronic charting system you choose should make it very clear to you which depth units are used by the chart you are viewing.**

Can I make my own charts?

There are some chart plotting products on the market that allow the user to scan in a portion of a paper navigational chart on a normal desktop scanning machine, and to display that on-screen. This concept is very appealing – generally speaking, once a navigator has purchased a paper chart, copyright law should not prevent him from scanning the chart *for personal use*, and using it with an electronic charting system.

A word of warning, however. The process by which paper charts are converted for use with computers is very involved. Correcting the scanned image for inaccuracies during the scanning process, 'warping' the scanned chart to match the correct map projection and correctly relating the electronic chart to a suitable geodetic datum, mean that an inexperienced individual may have problems producing electronic charts that are consistently accurate enough for safe navigation.

Of course, the choice is yours, but if you wish to 'make your own electronic charts' as opposed to purchasing those created by experienced cartographic professionals, you should at least be aware of the possible sources of error and navigate accordingly.

Updating electronic charts

Most chart producers offer updated versions of their charts at a reduced cost. Although you need to contact the chart suppliers direct for accurate quotations, it is usually possible to update an electronic chart you have bought for around one quarter of the new price.

Beware of the difference between Notice to Mariner (NM) corrections and chart re-issues (or new editions) though: usually, as with paper charts, there comes a point where it is not possible for the manufacturer to keep a chart up-to-date just by applying NM corrections. When this happens, the manufacturer usually withdraws the original chart and re-issues another (often with the same chart number, but with a different edition or issue number). As with paper charts, this may mean that you have effectively got to buy the electronic chart again at its full price, although some chart manufacturers will supply new editions/re-issues at a reduced price.

Some manufacturers offer updating services, on a weekly, monthly or quarterly basis, where they manage your chart portfolio for you and automatically send you chart updates, as and when they become due. These services are really aimed at commercial navigators and, due to the open-ended nature of these services, may prove quite costly for the leisure yachtsman if the charts covered have had many changes.

Each chart manufacturer has a different policy towards providing updated charts to users and the electronic chart marketplace is changing very quickly, so after taking the general advice above into account, it is wise to get specific advice from an experienced supplier at time of purchase.

Chart rotation

Often, a navigator will find it more convenient to rotate a paper chart so that he is viewing it 'heading up' or 'course up' or 'leg up', as opposed to the more usual 'North up'. If this feature is important to you, check how well systems cope with it because it is one of the more tricky areas for manufacturers to deal with. With raster charts it is not possible to rotate text so that it reads correctly whichever way up the chart is, but this is often possible with vector charting systems. If a vector system does rotate text, how is the rotation point handled, ie does the rotated text obscure the feature it is describing or other adjacent features? Ultimately, consider whether chart rotation actually enhances the usability of the chart.

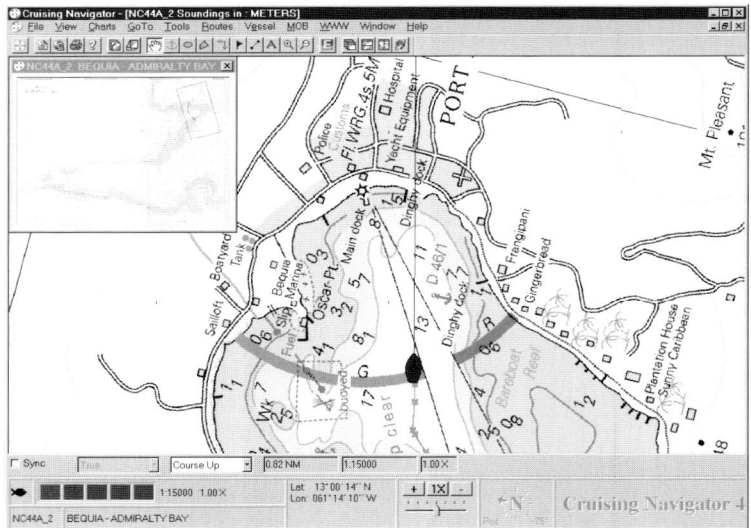

Chart rotation allows a charting system to mimic how a navigator may use paper charts in pilotage situations

Overzoom

The ability to 'overzoom' an electronic chart – that is, enlarge the image more than normal – can be very useful, especially on smaller PC displays. It can allow you to examine chart details more closely, or can help if the display is hard to see. Do make sure, though, that an overzooming system will display a prominent warning when in overzoom mode. This is because it would be very dangerous to look at an overzoomed smaller scale chart, believing it to be as accurate and as detailed as a larger scale chart.

Choosing an electronic charting system

Having decided which kind of electronic charts you wish to use, you should have automatically narrowed down the choice of electronic charting systems. Now it is time to look at the different kinds of electronic charting system and to discover the kinds of things to look for when choosing between them.

Planning or plotting?

There are really two main kinds of electronic charting systems. Firstly, and probably most obviously, is that of chart plotting. This is the simplest type: it takes the vessel's position from a suitable navigator and displays it on top of an electronic chart 'backdrop'. Chart plotting software may also keep an electronic log book of the vessel's position and display the vessel's historical track on the chart as well. This is an incredibly useful function that allows the navigator to keep a constant, accurate plot at all times. Of course, chart plotting software may perform other functions as well, but all will be associated with displaying the vessel's current position etc.

Full electronic charting systems perform all of the plotting functions as described above, but allow you to plan passages as well. Although the benefits of ordinary chart plotting are clear to see, the extra functions provided by full electronic charting systems make these very powerful systems, often for a small incremental cost.

Using an electronic charting system with planning capability means that the navigator can build up routes from lists of waypoints. If the electronic charting system includes tidal stream information, it will usually allow you to calculate the effect of the tide on your route as well. Some systems even provide an 'optimisation' capability, ie tell you the best time to leave to take maximum advantage of the tidal stream.

Waypoint navigation

Historically, small boat navigators within sight of land both planned and plotted their voyages by referring to chart features in relative terms, eg one mile due south of Bolt Head. Relative navigation is second nature to most navigators, but does require charted features to be visible to be of any use: it can be very difficult to return to a particular spot at night or in poor visibility purely by dead reckoning, or without radar.

Since GPS receivers have become common on board small vessels, many navigators have become familiar with the concept of waypoint navigation. A waypoint is quite simply a shorthand notation for a location you may wish to go to. A waypoint has two elements: a name and a position (expressed as latitude and longitude). GPS receivers usually have the ability to store and recall a limited number of waypoints – this can be very useful when wishing to go to, or return to, a particular location when visibility is poor. However, manipulating and using large numbers of waypoints can be challenging on the typical GPS receiver with a small screen and few buttons.

With PC-based systems, however, waypoint navigation really comes into its own. A large (often unlimited) number of waypoints with long, descriptive names may be stored on the PC's hard disk in different files and these waypoints can be easily built into routes. Some electronic charting systems are able to upload and download these waypoint lists to a suitable GPS receiver as well.

The following are all useful features that you might look out for when choosing an electronic charting system for your needs.

Multiple chart formats   As previously discussed, no one single electronic charting system has full worldwide coverage; therefore, to ensure widest possible coverage, it's important to purchase a system that can use more than one kind of electronic chart. This may not seem important if you usually cruise in just one area, but these days many people find themselves sailing further afield than they have expected, or go on charter holidays, where electronic chart coverage may differ from their home area.

It's wise to choose a system that lets you use raster charts and vector charts together so you can take advantage of the strengths of each type. For example, vector charts are particularly useful at smaller scales (say 1:100,000–1:1,000,000), where it is handy to be able to zoom in and out and to retain a clear chart display. In the authors' view, raster charts come into their own at scales of 1:75,000–1:20,000 and are ideal for harbour approaches and plans.

Multiple chart windows

One of the main problems with electronic charting systems on board at the current time is that of display size. A typical laptop PC screen may measure just 12.1" to 14" in size and will have a resolution of 800x600 or 1024x768 pixels. Even if a charting program is able to zoom in and zoom out (and particularly with raster charts), this means that the program will not be able to clearly display all of the electronic chart at once. A useful solution is to be able to divide the screen up into one or more 'windows'. Each window may contain an image of the same chart (or a different one), zoomed in by different amounts, which will allow the navigator to see not only the detail around the vessel, but the *context* of the voyage as well.

All in all, multiple chart windows are extremely useful and this feature should be placed pretty high up on the list of desirable features. Incidentally, one might assume that dividing an already small screen up into smaller windows would make the system less useful, but in fact this is not the case because each window contains more *useful* information than would a single chart window.

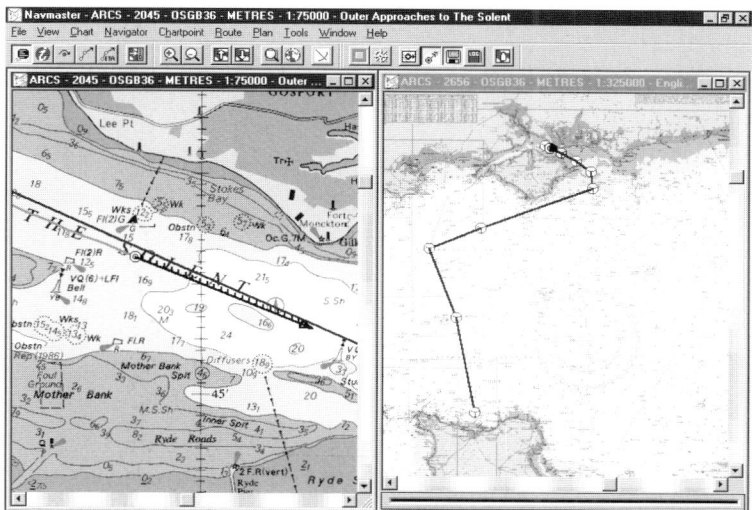

Multiple chart windows make good use of the available screen real-estate

Vessel following

Called by as many different names as there are manufacturers, this is a particularly useful feature whereby the system moves the electronic chart so as to keep the vessel symbol roughly centred on the chart. Some systems move the chart smoothly 'under' the vessel, others appear jerky and unnatural (especially on less powerful PCs). Many systems will change the chart automatically (or prompt you to load the next chart) when they reach the edge of the current chart in order to keep the vessel in view.

Look out for systems that let you change exactly *when* the chart scrolls and by how much; some systems let you 'look ahead' so you are viewing more of the chart in front of the vessel than behind.

For systems that offer multiple chart windows, check that it is possible to have some of them following the vessel and some of them not – that way, you can be planning this afternoon's passage in one window, whilst monitoring the current passage in another.

Autopilot control

Most chart plotting systems currently on the market claim to offer autopilot control as one of their features. Although the amount of control they offer varies between systems, usually they let you choose a course to steer on the PC and the system exports this to a suitable autopilot. Unless the autopilot is in standby mode, it should immediately try to bring the vessel round to the selected course. Some systems will automatically instruct the autopilot to change course once a waypoint is reached (or at least when the vessel gets within a user-selected distance from the waypoint).

> **Important Note** – Autopilot control is a very useful function, though it must be stressed that a good lookout should be kept at all times – it would be very dangerous to rely solely on an autopilot, especially in crowded waters or close to other hazards.

Bearing and distance calculation

When navigating using paper charts, distances are usually measured off the vertical scale on the chart using a pair of dividers. This is not possible with electronic charting systems because of the way charts are displayed on-screen, so even the most basic system should provide tools which will let you measure the distance between two points.

More advanced systems will also display the bearing and the reciprocal between two points or allow you to quickly measure between several points at once. Some will even display measured distances according to rhumb line or great circle methods.

Routes

Virtually all systems allow you to build routes from the program's internal database(s) of waypoints, or by placing them graphically onto the chart with the mouse cursor. A route is simply a named list of waypoints, but look out for useful features such as the ability to reverse a route, or make a quick route from the vessel's current position. You should be allowed to annotate each route file and be able to save, copy, rename and delete them without having to leave the program. If it is important to you, look out for the ability to upload a complete route into a GPS, which can provide a useful back-up should your PC fail while at sea.

Tidal passage planning

With the exception of the most basic systems, electronic charting programs will allow you to calculate the effect of tidal streams on your intended route. It works like this: choose a series of waypoints to define your intended route, then choose a date and time of departure and a realistic vessel speed. Working from the PC's internal clock and the program's built-in tidal information, it will apply the effect of the tidal stream on your route and will be able to display not only the expected time of arrival, but also an expected ground track. More advanced systems also allow you to find out the best time to leave to take maximum advantage of the tides.

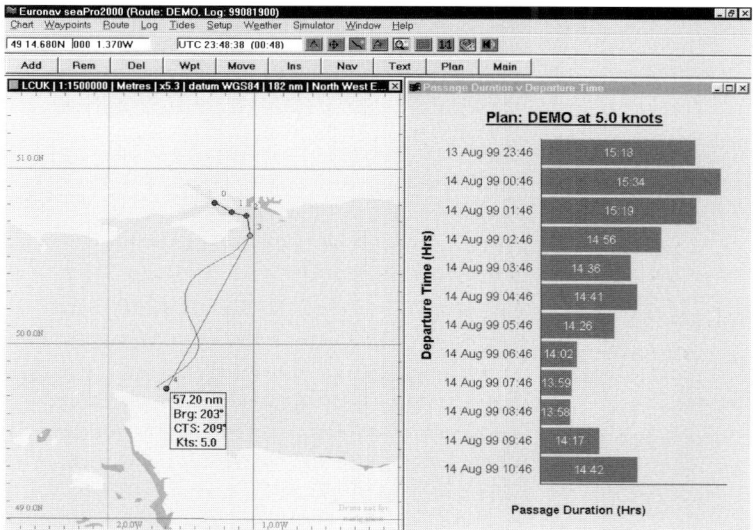

seaPro 2000's passage planning and route optimisation facilities

Of course, we rarely sail to planned speed and sailing boats often can't make the desired course, so look out for the ability to easily re-plan the rest of the route from your current position. Other features worth having for sailing boats are the ability to choose different speeds for each leg of the route and to allow a leeway factor for each leg.

There are so many variables affecting a small boat at sea that it would be unreasonable to expect these tidal passage plans to be really accurate. However, the more accurate they are the better, so consider the quality and coverage of any included tidal stream data. Some programs include tidal stream data free of charge, but for a limited area – if you sail outside of this area, how will you obtain more tidal data? Can you purchase a disk or must you type the data in?

Some manufacturers advertise their system's ability to perform tidal passage planning, but don't actually include any data; remember to cost this in when you are comparing systems from different manufacturers. Also consider that some systems require an annual update to the tidal information, without which the tidal functions either won't work, or may be much less accurate. ·

Finally, consider where the tidal stream data comes from in the first place. Private organisations as well as hydrographic offices provide tidal stream data; some is produced using mathematical models rather than observations. This is one area where it will really pay to do some solid research before deciding on a system. If in doubt, consult a marine computing specialist since a manufacturer may not be in a position to offer truly impartial advice.

Tidal heights   There are several programs available that will work out times and heights of high and low water in various places (see next chapter). Whilst these are very useful pieces of software in their own right, it is certainly far more convenient to have this functionality built in to an electronic charting system. In any case, if the charting system is able to perform passage planning, taking into account tidal streams, it is very easy for the manufacturer to provide this function as well.

Dead reckoning   Since a chart plotting system by definition requires an electronic navigator input, it may seem odd to include a dead reckoning (DR) facility. The main reason this is important is if your navigator or its antenna should fail or if for some other reason a GPS signal is not available to the charting system.

A DR mode should allow you to choose a vessel location, course and speed and display the vessel symbol as if a GPS were connected. Provision of this useful facility varies between systems – some don't provide it at all; some do, but charge extra for it; and some include it as standard.

> **Important Note** – If the system you are considering does offer a DR facility, check whether it is automatically activated should the GPS fail. If so, it is *absolutely essential* that the system makes it very obvious it is operating in DR mode. The danger of course is that an automatic DR mode won't take into account actual course and speed changes and could therefore be showing the vessel in the wrong position.

Manual plotting

In case your GPS does fail, far more important than a DR facility is the ability to lay down observed bearings onto the electronic chart and to add a manually entered position within the resulting 'cocked hat'. It may also be desirable to be able to plot a line of position (LOP) derived from astro navigation. This manual log entry should have a manual 'time stamp' and it should be possible to expand on it with narrative text.

Look out for manual plotting tools that give you range and bearings from and to objects, that allow you to work in degrees true or magnetic and, above all, that are easy to use – if they're unfriendly, you won't play with them; if you don't play with them, you won't know how to operate them when you need to.

Man overboard

There are two schools of thought when it comes to man overboard (MOB) features on electronic charting systems. The first is that it is a very useful feature that may help to save life; the second is that the last thing anyone should be doing in a man overboard scenario is trying to remember how to activate the charting system's man overboard function.

Clearly both schools have their merit, but to help you decide whether this is important for you, try to mentally follow the procedure through should you ever find yourself in this situation. If the charting system in question makes it **very easy** to record a MOB position and **automatically** provides **useful** information to help return to the casualty's last known position, it may be considered worthwhile, as long as all on board are fully trained in its use. If not, it simply isn't worth considering.

Some charting systems provide automatic search pattern generation which could be useful when planning an extended search and rescue operation; however, in the authors' opinion there has yet to be designed a simple and useful system that really offers more than the MOB button found on most GPS receivers.

Logging

Basic chart plotting programs simply display incoming NMEA0183 data such as the vessel's position. More advanced systems are able to save this data into a log file as well. If logging is important to you (maybe for race analysis), look out for systems that will also allow you to log other data – for example, true and apparent wind, depth and water temperature etc. The best systems allow you to choose the frequency with which data is written to the log file – this is important because logged NMEA0183 data can quickly build up into very large files on your PC's hard disk. Is the logging frequency the same for every incoming data item or can you record each type of data at different frequencies?

Win LOG — 06/10/99 — 06/10/99 15:37

START TIME 14:30:27   END TIME 14:58:49   STEP 1 min.

Time	Apparent wind angle (AVG deg)	Apparent wind speed (AVG kn)	True wind angle (AVG deg)	True wind direction (AVG deg)	True wind speed (AVG kn)	Wind direction over ground (AVG deg)	Wind speed over ground (AVG kn)
14:58:49	65	4.04	158	203	9.61	197	9.01
14:58:27	62	4.7	153	196	9.23	196	9.68
14:57:27	70	5.21	149	191	9.45	190	9.58
14:56:27	69	5.51	146	186	9.24	186	9.55
14:55:27	69	5.55	144	188	8.82	186	8.98
14:54:27	62	4.86	149	189	8.39	188	8.41
14:53:27	55	4.56	154	200	8.51	200	8.95
14:52:27	53	5.96	144	197	8.14	199	8.22
14:51:27	54	5.47	146	200	7.99	200	8.33
14:50:27	53	6.01	140	194	7.54	192	7.5
14:49:27	55	5.91	141	193	7.63	190	7.92
14:48:27	61	5.99	142	192	8.41	192	8.95
14:47:27	57	5.94	142	191	8.01	190	8
14:46:27	56	4.67	150	196	7.68	194	7.95
14:45:27	58	3.2	161	209	8.53	210	8.79
14:44:27	59	4.52	153	199	8.56	197	9.01
14:43:27	49	4.29	154	201	7.46	205	7.69
14:42:27	51	3.91	157	206	7.68	204	8.01
14:41:27	48	4.69	152	204	7.43	207	7.48
14:40:27	48	5.66	146	199	7.51	198	7.7
14:39:27	48	4.06	157	209	7.75	211	8.03
14:38:27	47	5.35	149	202	7.53	203	7.79
14:37:27	48	5.21	149	199	7.56	201	7.91
14:36:27	48	4.32	155	200	7.64	198	7.96
14:35:27	50	2.98	163	208	7.91	206	7.76
14:34:27	61	2.73	163	209	8.23	207	8.6
14:33:27	71	2.59	164	209	8.96	210	8.87
14:32:27	73	3.12	162	208	9.39	208	9.67
14:31:27	66	4.15	155	199	9.06	200	9.56
14:30:27	60	4	157	202	8.72	....	....

Logging incoming NMEA data is very useful for performance analysis

Simply logging incoming instrument data is all very well, but to be of any use the log must also allow the navigator to add manual, narrative log entries.

One other very useful function is the ability to play back the log of a particular voyage or to display a previous voyage track if you wish to retrace your steps.

Overlaying data

Only the most basic electronic charting systems prevent you from 'drawing' on the electronic chart. The ability to mark areas to avoid, or to clearly mark dangers, is almost essential in a system to be used on board. Some systems have simple and easy to use 'free-hand' drawing ability, whilst others offer comprehensive but much more complex line, arc, point and polygon drawing tools, even using multiple layers as in a graphics program. Look out for the ability to save and load your overlay files to disk, acquaint yourself with the user interface – even if the overlay function is powerful, if it's difficult to use, then you'll avoid using it.

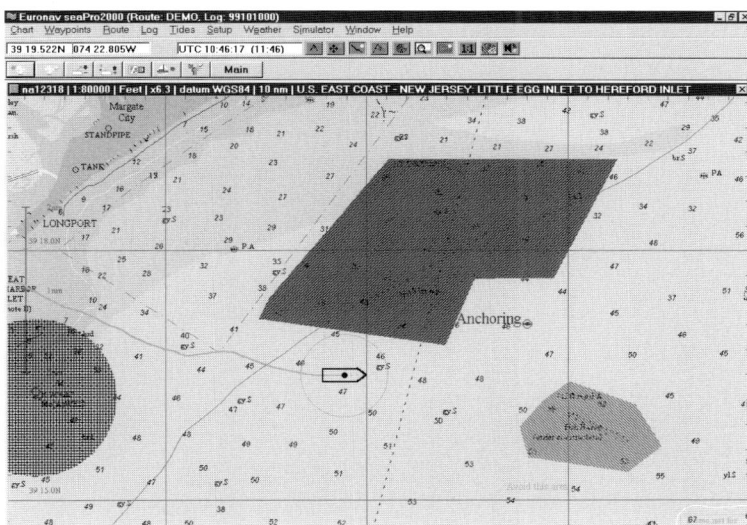

Overlays allow you to mark your own point, line and area information on the chart

One very popular use of overlay functions is the ability to build up your own pilotage notes. Text, scanned-in pictures, even video sequences, may be attached to 'hotspots' overlaid onto the electronic chart. When queried (usually by pointing at the hotspot and clicking with the mouse), the system should pop up a box showing the stored text, with buttons to view any attached pictures or video files. One of the most difficult things in the past was adding pictures to the system, but today's digital cameras and camcorders make this really easy.

Alarm zones

Several of the electronic charting systems currently available allow the user to add one or more alarm zones to the chart. This involves drawing an area (or, in simple systems, a circle) which, when the vessel enters or leaves it, triggers an alarm condition. Depending

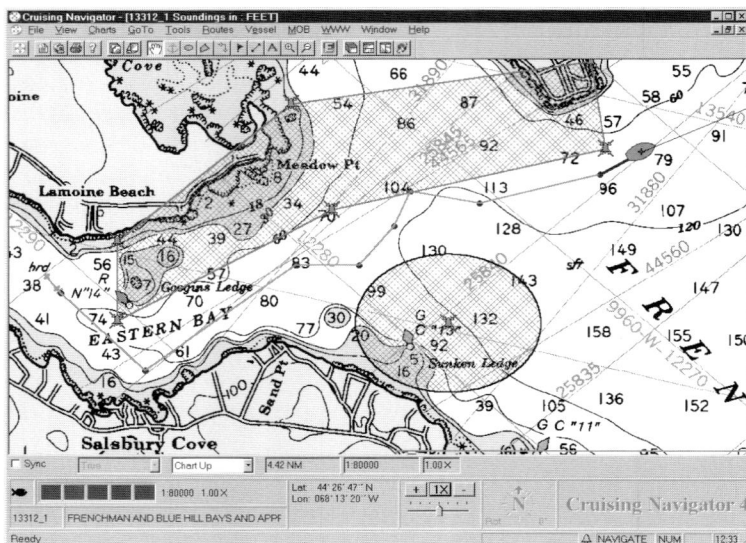

Alarm zones can be set to activate when the vessel enters or leaves them and should present visual and audible warnings

upon the system, the alarm may simply involve the display of a flashing button, or may use the PC's sound card to play an audible alarm. Bear in mind that unless you have powerful speakers attached to your PC (that are switched on!), an audible alarm may be difficult to hear over background noises, so rely on this feature with caution and make sure that the system provides a really noticeable visual alarm as well.

Some systems advertise the ability to build up alarm zones automatically, on the basis of depth for example. Be wary of this feature – it's all very well if the chart data you are using is accurate enough, but this is often difficult to rely on, particularly with smaller scale charts. Much better to let the system highlight all depths shallower than 6 metres (for example) and then to use the system's alarm zone tools to draw in your own alarm boundaries.

Radar and ARPA radar overlay

Until fairly recently, ARPA radar sets were the preserve of commercial vessels only; however, a steady reduction in cost means that ARPA radars should become quite common in the 11 metre (35 feet) and upwards bracket. In a traditional radar set, transmitted signals are bounced back to the vessel and are shown on the radar display as a series of blips. ARPA radars include powerful software that analyses patterns in the returned blips and highlights them as 'targets'. With a GPS set connected, the ARPA radar software is able to cancel out own vessel movement and highlight targets that are moving relative to the vessel and to the land. An ARPA radar set applies identification numbers to each target and some of these sets are able to export these via NMEA0183. Along with the target vessel's identifier number, its position, course and speed, an ARPA radar may also export useful collision-avoidance information for each target, such as the closest point of approach and the time to closest point of approach.

Recently, we have seen dedicated raster scan radar packages appearing. These incorporate a scanner head, electronics drivers and a computer interface card and are designed to replace a standard dedicated radar unit.

Night vision

Many system manufacturers claim to offer night vision capabilities. This is usually a choice of 'day', 'dusk' and 'night' settings, with the latter changing the colours of the display so as not to damage a navigator's night vision. Don't be satisfied with the manufacturers' claims though, because some systems only dim the electronic chart and fail to make the area surrounding the screen dim as well. A perfectly dimmed electronic chart is less than useless if the rest of the system makes you feel as if someone is shining a high-powered torch into your eyes – check that the system actually dims the Windows 'system colours' as well as just the chart window.

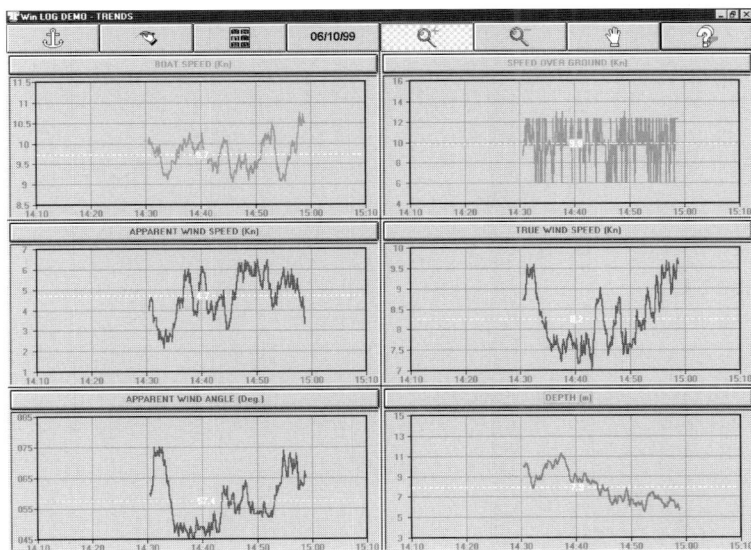

Real-time logging and graphing is invaluable for performance sailing (see page 42)

Log graphing

Log graphing allows you to see incoming NMEA0183 data graphically. This is particularly useful for performance sailing where you can compare two or more parameters together, which makes it far easier to spot trends as they happen. Examples might be wind shifts or poor helming affecting the course or speed.

As well as being able to display incoming data in real-time, it can also be very useful to graph data off-line for performance analysis. The more powerful systems allow you to load up a previously recorded log file and to display the data in graph form. Some systems allow you to choose different graph types to help visualise different kinds of data more easily.

Sailing functions

Sailing boat navigators, particularly race boat navigators, have a number of specific extra requirements. Programs offering these functions have been available for use by competitors in events such as the *America's Cup* and *Admiral's Cup*, but are now becoming available in more mainstream programs.

The key factors are concerned with boats sailing at different speeds on different points of sail, and of course not being able to sail directly into the wind. The program will have a model of the boat's performance, her polars, and use this to predict the speed on each leg, tacking and gybing laylines into the mark, and sometimes even

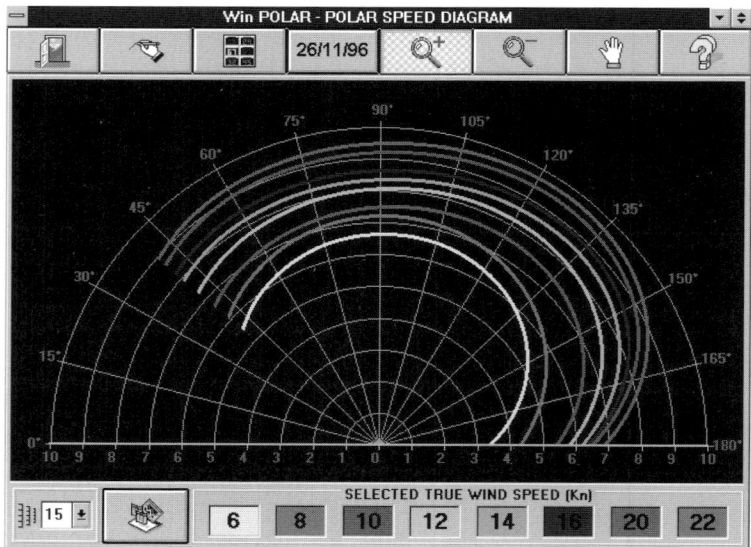

A boat's polar table(s) let the navigator know how well the boat is doing against her optimum performance

the fastest route to the next waypoint. More sophisticated programs will also allow the navigator to monitor performance, and to experiment with different wind conditions.

Of obvious use for racing sailors, polars can also be useful for cruising yachtsmen – when we are sailing, how confident are we that we are doing as well as could be, or should be, for the conditions?

Fuel calculations

Tidal passage planning is certainly less important for semi-displacement/planing powered craft than it is for sailing boats, but some electronic charting systems will work out fuel consumption as well. The power boat owner types in the vessel's fuel consumption characteristics and this, together with the fuel cost per litre, lets him quickly work out the cost of a particular trip and so allows him to save money by working the tides to his advantage.

Interfacing

When evaluating systems, consider how well the software system copes with interfacing to a navigator and other on board instruments. Some systems will simply take NMEA0183 position information for plotting, others will 'understand' and use a wide variety of types of data, and some will even export or repeat data for other instruments (such as an autopilot or a radar) to use. Even if a system copes with a wide variety of data types, you should also consider how easy it is to set it up – this is an area that can be fraught with difficulties if the software you are using is 'unfriendly'. There are systems on the market that not only have comprehensive interfacing controls, but are also simple to set up, even being provided with tools to automatically analyse incoming data and to suggest an optimum set-up.

One thing is certain, most interfacing problems are caused by poor quality electrical connections between the 'talker' (eg GPS set) and the 'listener' (eg the PC's serial port). More information on this is to be found in chapter 10; success is largely in your hands, but it's worth pointing out that some system manufacturers supply a 'plain' serial cable, whereas others provide a proper shielded opto-isolated interface cable. The latter costs a bit more to provide, but nine times out of ten will solve physical interfacing problems that may be experienced with a plain serial cable.

Above, we refer to cables in the singular – in fact, you will usually have to deal with two cables, since most smaller GPS sets are fitted with proprietary connectors. Unless you have a suitable connector to plug into the GPS set, you will need to buy the manufacturer's own cable (often this same cable is used to get 12VDC power from the boat's supply). You connect the GPS cable's signal wires to those of the charting system's cable. Most manufacturers supply sufficient information for you to do this yourself, but you must make good connections – you *can* use 'chocolate block' type connectors, but as with all marine electrical connections, you are advised to solder and seal the connections for trouble-free operation.

In summary

The aforementioned points are really only scratching the surface with modern electronic charting systems. There are clearly many factors that may influence your decision as to which product to purchase, and as systems develop and manufacturers become more competitive, this process will get more complicated.

We have seen that it is best to decide on what kinds of charts you wish to use first, and to look at the features of the electronic charting system itself later. The real message has to be that you must 'try before you buy' since each system has differing user interfaces as well as capabilities. To this end, most manufacturers provide demonstration CD-ROMs which you can install on your PC and evaluate the system at your leisure. Better still, book a training session with a marine computing specialist, where you will be able to try several systems as well as pick the brains of experienced and impartial professionals.

Although to many yachtsmen computer navigation is synonymous with electronic charting, there are other areas where computer power is useful in assisting traditional navigation techniques, without going over completely to electronic charting. Examples worthy of mention are tide height prediction and astro navigation programs. You may also consider using an 'electronic almanac' that replicates the information found in traditional paper publications, using the PC's multimedia capabilities to present the information in a format that is easy to access and understand.

Tide height prediction

Whether or not you take your PC on board, a tide height prediction program can make life so much easier, and the computerised version is actually cheaper than buying tide tables each year.

Simply select the location you want the tidal data for, and the range of dates, to bring up a graphical or tabulated tidal curve. It is very simple to identify the tidal height for a given date and time, or to

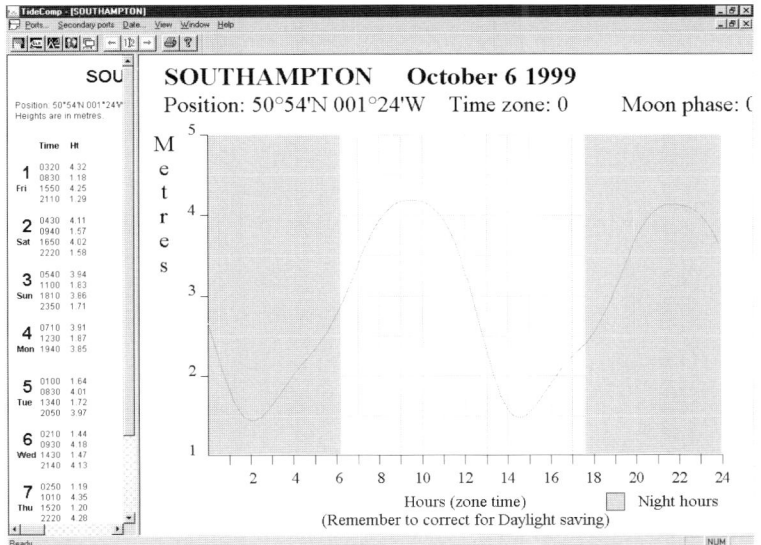

Tide height prediction programs are usually based on the same data as is used in printed almanacs

work the other way round and to find out at what time a required tidal height occurs.

Several of the programs currently available have a perpetual almanac and provide reasonably accurate calculations until the year 2100. Some programs also allow you to enter your boat's draft and mast height, together with charted depths and air clearances, and so can calculate clearance times for bridges and underwater obstructions.

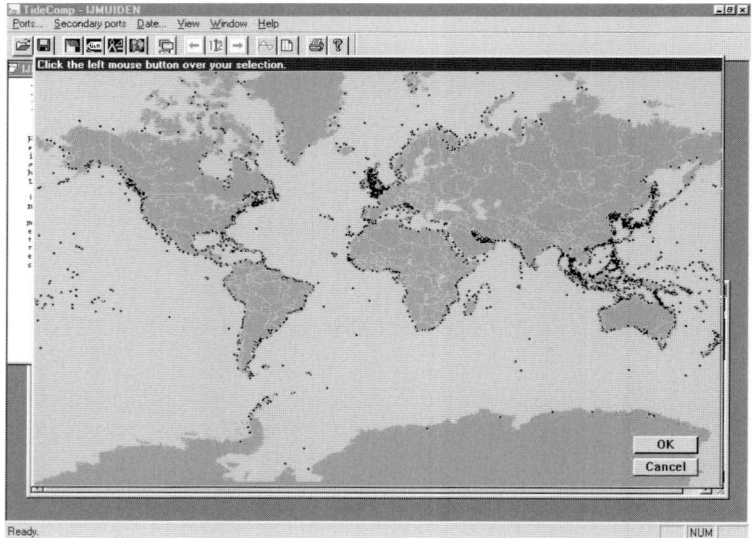

Many tide programs can give access to tidal height information covering over 4,500 primary and secondary ports worldwide

Too good to be true?

The big problem in predicting tides is that the heights are very dependent on atmospheric conditions, local geography, river flows etc. These factors have such a great effect on the actual amount of water available at a given time that all tidal height predictions (whether computer-based or tabulated in a printed almanac) should only be taken as a guide. Indeed, a purely theoretical/mathematical approach cannot be used. Additionally, tide heights are monitored over a period of time – ideally a full year but often a matter of weeks or days – and predictions are based on analyses of these observations.

One of the most obvious factors affecting tidal height is the wind – in time a wind will move water from the windward to the leeward shore. Barometric pressure also has a significant effect – an increase in pressure will reduce the height of tide. In a river, heavy rainfall upstream will work its way down the river, resulting in raised water levels. On a larger scale, some shallow confined seas, such as the North Sea, can have storm surges when the right combination of weather conditions occur.

There are a number of methods of predicting tides: in most waters, **harmonic analysis** gives the best results. Here various cyclical astronomical coefficients are modelled by a number of factors. Each factor has a cyclical period; and a time lag and amplitude, derived from observations. Astronomical coefficients vary in period from about 4 hours to 19 years.

In some waters, such as shallow estuaries, a standing wave can be set up in the estuary, causing further oscillations in tide heights. In the harmonic method this is modelled by a number of shallow water coefficients. However, in extreme cases, such as in some German waters, better results are obtained by using non-harmonic prediction methods.

The **Simplified Harmonic Method** (SHM) is an approximation of the Full Harmonic Method (FHM) that makes calculations much quicker with a relatively minor reduction in accuracy. It takes the groups of similar coefficients and consolidates them into four main coefficients, adjusted for astronomical factors. It also includes shallow water effects, and monthly seasonal variations in sea level and coefficients.

In printed tide tables, there are usually a small number of **primary ports** with pre-computed heights, where generally there has been at least a year's observations, and **secondary ports**. For each secondary port, a primary port with a similar tidal curve is selected as a base, and then time and height corrections are given relative to the primary port. This is a convenience for the navigator without a PC, and the results are generally less accurate than using the SHM.

Most tide prediction programs are based on the SHM, which is mostly accurate to about 0.1 metres for primary ports. Some PC programs or those for hand-held computers may use a reduced set of coefficients, and so be less accurate.

Other programs use the **Full Harmonic Method** (FHM), which offers greater theoretical accuracy than the SHM. In addition to the four primary factors, these systems may use over a hundred secondary factors for some locations (many of these may have only a minimal effect on the accuracy of the predictions). However, when one considers the additional cost of the data FHM systems require and all the external sources of inaccuracy – wind strength and direction, atmospheric pressure, river flow and so on – these systems are seldom recommended for normal leisure use.

Tidal passage planning

Though many yachtsmen would like to run a full-blown electronic charting system on their PC, there are also those who prefer not to take a newer or more powerful PC on board; indeed, there are still many older PCs in regular use on board that are not powerful enough to run today's electronic charting software. Some yachtsmen even argue that since they have a built-in dedicated chart plotter on their boat, they have no need for PC style high-quality electronic charts, but would still like a hand with tidal passage planning and don't see why they should pay the premium for the latest, high powered electronic charting system.

Fortunately, there is software available that was designed to run on older, less powerful computers. This software will perform simple tidal passage planning and optimisation functions, even displaying an expected ground track for a given boat speed and departure time. Even if not used on board, such a system will allow the navigator to print out a succinct plan of their route before going to sea. Some of these systems will also perform positional plotting from a GPS set whilst at sea, albeit on very basic, simplified charts.

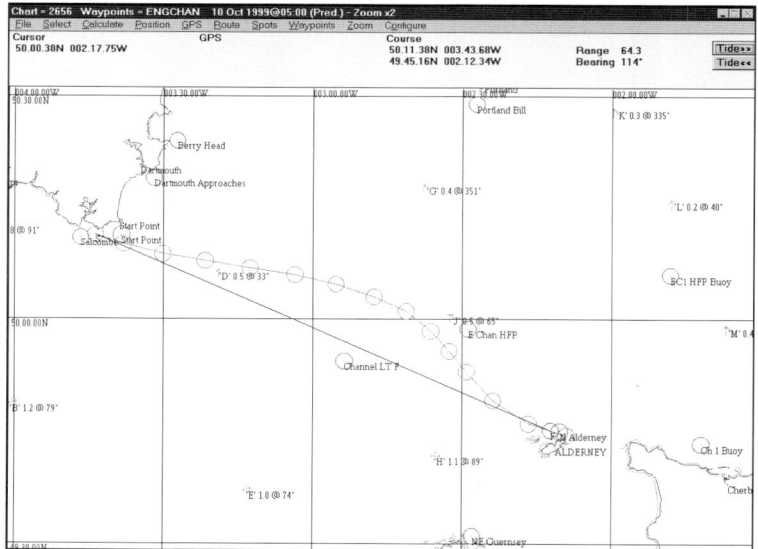

Even simpler, low-cost systems may offer advanced facilities, such as tidal passage planning

Almanacs

Another kind of program that is incredibly useful on board, as well as at home prior to going to sea, is an electronic almanac. This kind of product is born from the idea that the tabulated information commonly found in a printed almanac is bulky and awkward to use. Combining all the information relevant to a yachtsman into one consistent user interface on the PC makes it much more easy and convenient to access.

An electronic almanac may include an enormous range of functions and information sources, including chart plotting and logging, tidal heights and streams, pilotage notes and weather and radio information. If it is well designed, so it is easy to find the desired information, this can be a very useful utility; more so if it elegantly interfaces to a chart plotting system.

Bear in mind that there will probably be ongoing costs associated with an electronic almanac – it will usually be purchased containing information for just one region or area, and if you wish to use it in a different area, you will need to purchase add-on area information. Similarly, much of the information found in a program like this must be considered perishable and will almost certainly need updating annually.

As with commercial 'office type' suites of applications, it is unlikely that one 'heavyweight' almanac program will suit all users equally.

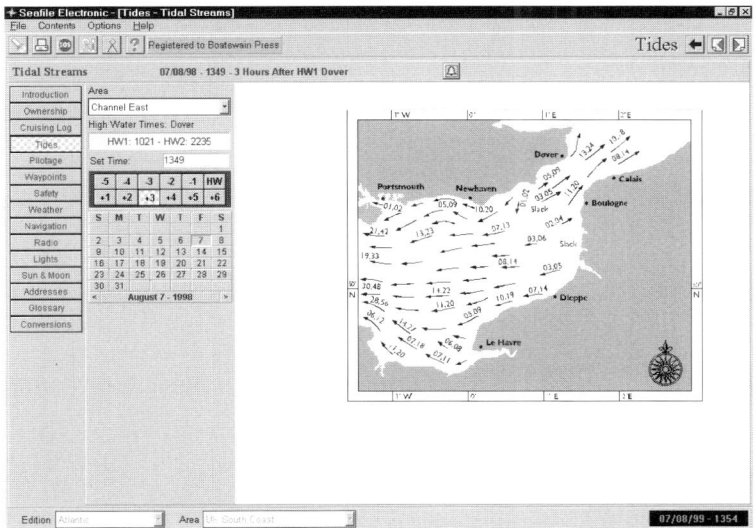

Electronic almanacs show information from printed almanacs, but in an easy to access format

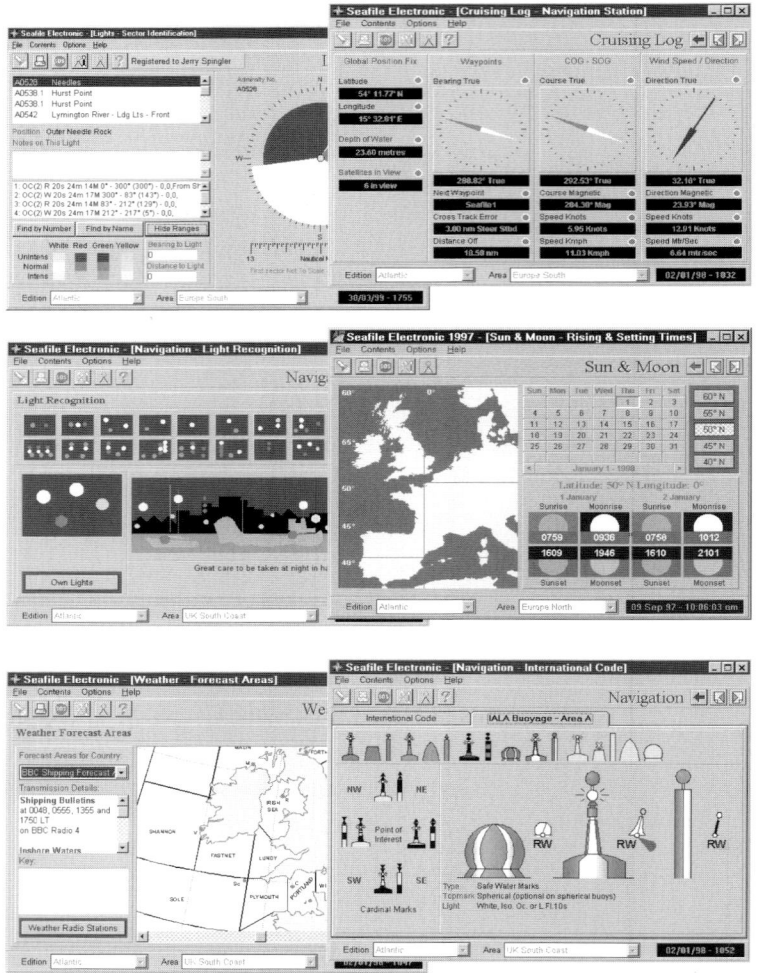

Almanac programs contain a wealth of useful information, but the key to their success lies in the ease with which information can be accessed

To this end, an electronic almanac should allow the user to 'plug in' some of their own favourite components, should the included ones prove not to their taste. This is especially the case if the electronic almanac also has a built-in chart plotter – check that this can be disabled and replaced with your favourite system.

Although some limited almanac-type information is now becoming available built in to electronic charts, always consider the source of the data – does it come from a respected publisher? Generally speaking, if you are satisfied with the quality and detail of the information contained in your usual paper almanac, the chances are that an electronic version of the same information will be more useful to you than one based on other sources.

If an electronic almanac system is going to be truly useful, you may well become dependent upon it. Check candidate systems thoroughly for reliability – do they cause problems with the operation of your chart plotting program, for example? Finally, **never** be tempted to go to sea without an up-to-date printed almanac and pilotage information on board; even if you use your electronic almanac most of the time, make sure you can revert to traditional methods easily should you need to.

Astro navigation

Whilst almost everyone uses GPS as a primary means of navigation, for those who venture offshore it is still useful to be able to revert to astro when required, to safeguard against a damaged GPS receiver/antenna or poor signal reception. It is worth mentioning that GPS signals can be inadvertently jammed by sources such as TV transmitters, as well as intentional jamming tests occasionally carried out by the military. And for many there is just the pleasure of mastering a traditional method of navigation.

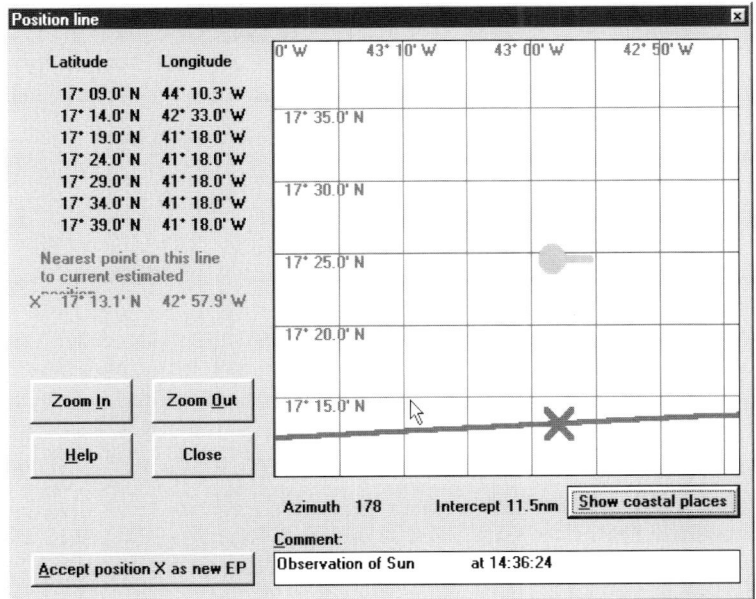

A line of position is easily plotted by the computer from its built-in ephemera and the navigator's sextant sight

Astronomical Observation

17° 24.6' N	42° 58.4' W	25 November 96 GMT 14:36:24

Name	Azimuth	Altitude	Brightness
Sun	178	51° 13.6'	0.0
Moon	260	23° 15.1'	1.0
Venus	128	24° 47.2'	2.1
Jupiter	227	48° 41.3'	5.2
Mercury	157	46° 00.4'	5.2
Vega	038	61° 32.2'	7.0
Arcturus	295	43° 42.9'	7.0
Rigil_Kent	208	8° 36.9'	7.0
Hadar	213	4° 52.3'	7.6
Altair	106	55° 35.2'	7.8
Spica	261	24° 06.5'	8.0

Observe...   Help   Advanced >>   Close

Sort list on: ● Brightness ○ Azimuth ○ Altitude ○ Name

Most programs contain extensive ephemera – details of all the heavenly bodies that are commonly used in astro navigation

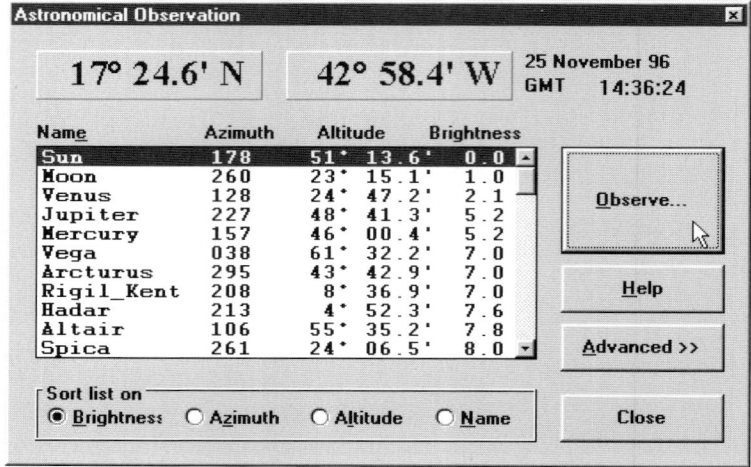

The drawback for many lies not so much in the use of the sextant, but in the volumes of tables and multitude of arithmetical operations needed to obtain a line of position (LOP). Though not difficult, there are many stages involved in obtaining an accurate LOP, and unless one regularly practises the procedure, it is very easy to make errors that will render the LOP hopelessly inaccurate.

Using a sight reduction program on the PC can make life much easier. Some, such as *Win Astro*, run on a PC, but others run on hand-held devices such as the Psion and the new Windows CE palmtop computers. In all cases, though, their operation is similar:

Sextant

Sun

GMT of observation
14:36:24   Set time...
☐ Real time

Observed sextant altitude: (uncorrected) **51** degrees **14** mins

Sextant corrections
Height of eye: 6.5 feet   ○ Upper edge observed
Index error -2 mins   ● Lower edge observed

Computed corrections (mins)
Dip: -2.5   Semi-diameter +16.3
Parallax +0.1   Refraction -0.8
Corrected altitude: 51° 25.1'

Show position line   Help   Cancel

The navigator enters observed data into a 'form'; the computer uses this information to produce a line of position

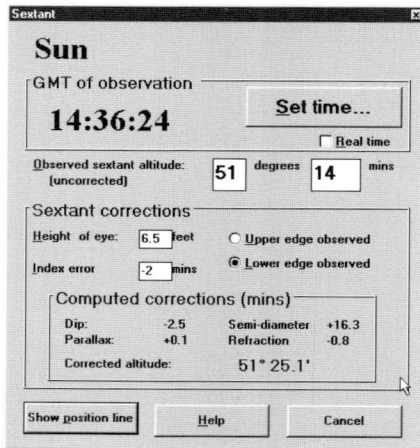

From a dead reckoning (DR) position the program will use its built-in almanac to give the positions of various celestial bodies as an altitude (height) and azimuth (bearing). You then select a body to take a sight on, enter the time and sextant altitude, and the PC will give you a line of position. No more messing about with tables, and the result is available in just seconds.

4 • Communications

For many of us, one of the main pleasures involved in recreational boating is in 'getting away from it all'. For others, though, it is very important to be able to keep in touch with loved ones whilst away sailing. Increasingly, as modern communications technologies have become much more affordable and reliable, many of us are able to justify spending more time on the boat because we can keep in touch with the office. Indeed, it is not unknown nowadays for an individual to be able to run a business entirely from on board their boat.

Radio or satcom?

Most yachtsmen will have encountered VHF (Very High Frequency) radio at some time or other, and will be familiar with the fact that it's range is limited to line-of-sight. Without delving too deeply into radio theory, this range is due to the fact that VHF radio waves (marine VHF uses 156MHz) travel in a straight line and are unable to follow the curvature of the earth. This results in VHF radio having a typical range of around 20–30 miles, depending upon the height and gain of the transmitting and receiving antennas as well as transmitter power.

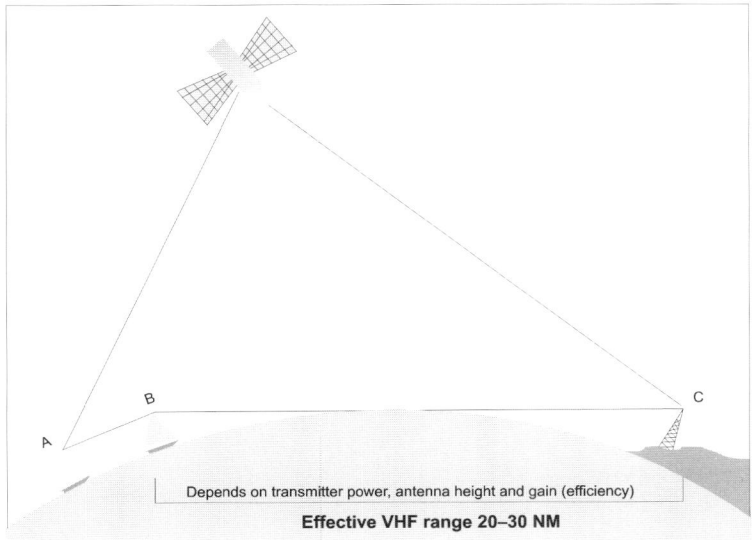

Using VHF, vessel B can communicate with radio station C, but because of the curvature of the earth, A is out of range. She could still communicate with the land however, via satellite

Depends on transmitter power, antenna height and gain (efficiency)

Effective VHF range 20–30 NM

This is not very far for those going offshore and, until recent times, all mariners venturing outside the range of VHF have had to fit either Medium Frequency (MF) or High Frequency (HF) Single Side Band (SSB) radio sets to stay in touch with the land or with distant vessels. Although MF/HF can give worldwide coverage, working these frequencies is very tricky and is notoriously unreliable due to changes in environmental factors. Indeed, until fairly recently, commercial vessels carried a dedicated radio officer, and to have an MF/HF SSB radio on board a small yacht was unusual.

SSB sets have improved immensely over the last ten years or so and they have become far more popular with yachtsmen (especially blue-water sailors). But the biggest improvement in communications has been with the introduction of satellite-based communication systems.

Instead of trying to communicate over vast distances with MF and HF radio, satellite communications (satcom) systems work over the same line-of-sight principles as VHF – signals are beamed over Ultra High Frequency (UHF) to a satellite that is in view above the horizon. From there, the signal is beamed back down to a 'land earth station', from where it is linked to its destination over the normal international telephone network. As long as a sufficient number of satellites are in the sky, satcom systems offer high-quality, reliable and global communications.

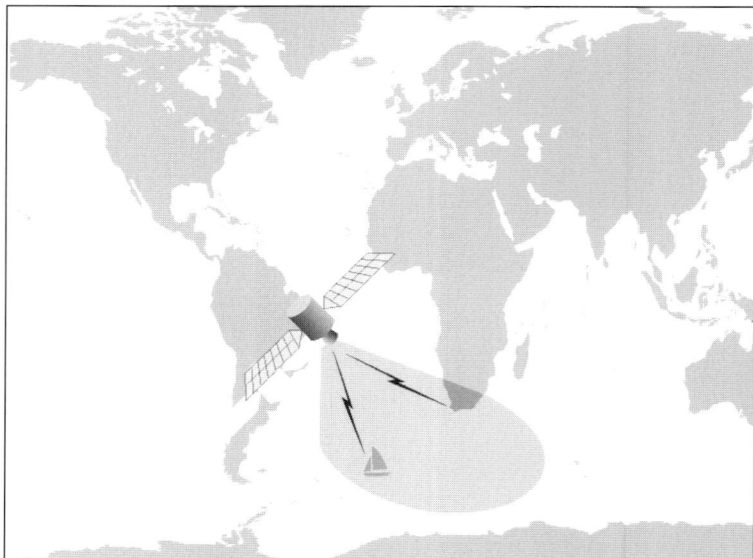

Satellite 'footprint' – both the vessel and 'land earth station' must have a satellite in view to permit simultaneous two-way communications

On the face of it, one wonders why the mariner bothers with anything other than satcom systems for general correspondence – the answer, of course, has been cost. However, if the greater installation costs of an SSB radio are included, nowadays there is little to choose between a system such as INMARSAT C and an SSB installation, though higher performance satcom units are still relatively expensive.

For convenience, communications systems can be divided into two groups, which we'll call *phone-based systems* and *messaging systems*. Phone-based systems give you essentially the same voice, fax and data services as a normal land telephone line (though sometimes with limitations). Messaging systems are simpler, allowing text-based e-mail, telex or other messages to be transmitted.

Satellite v Radio Communications

Choosing between 'traditional' radio communications and satellite communications is not simply a matter of cost, although most choices will have an effect on cost. The following should all be considered when making this difficult choice.

◆ **Coverage** – which services are available in the parts of the world you will be sailing in?

◆ **Range required** – the distance which needs to be covered to coast radio stations or other vessels.

◆ **Distress facility** – if distress facilities are required, which they normally are, it makes good sense to use the same system for general communications where possible.

◆ **Type of transmission** – voice, fax, electronic mail (e-mail) or telex.

◆ **Security** – is the information to be transmitted confidential or not?

◆ **Cost** – consider both initial purchase cost and ongoing or 'airtime' costs. Also consider alternative uses to which the equipment may be put, for example, a blue-water yachtsman may use an SSB radio for global e-mail, weatherfax, spoken weather forecasts, as well as (free) spoken communication with other SSB equipped yachts.

◆ **Convenience and reliability** – using SSB is inexpensive, but is much more complicated to operate than just 'picking up the phone'.

◆ **Data rate** or **bandwidth** – these terms refer to the amount of information which can be transferred concurrently. Typically, low bandwidth systems may be suitable for telex or e-mail, whereas sending pictures or video footage would require a high bandwidth.

ICOM's PCR1000 SSB receiver does not need a front panel as it is completely controlled by a PC

Use with PCs   Some communications systems require the use of a PC on board. Even with those that do not, adding a PC can enhance the system you are using, often saving communications charges or allowing you to transmit and receive other useful types of data. Using a PC keyboard is often more convenient than typing on the communications unit itself and a PC will allow you to save, print and organise your files much more easily.

Some radios are now designed exclusively for operation with a PC – having a 'virtual' control panel. As well as the obvious cost savings to the manufacturer, these PC-driven radios can be far more convenient to install, protect and operate than their predecessors.

Phone communication systems

These systems give the same range of facilities as a normal land-based phone line. The most familiar is the cellular mobile phone, but this category also incorporates satellite systems such as INMARSAT A, B and Mini-M, and newer satellite services that are coming on-stream currently eg Teledesic.

Fax services   Sending a fax via phone-based communications systems is the same as using a fax modem on a land-based phone line. You prepare the document on your word processor, and then simply select 'Fax' as the printer, either typing in the fax number or selecting it from an address book. The same fax driver software will receive incoming faxes (so long as the PC is running and the phone is not being used for anything else at the time). However, as with a land line, the incoming fax is received as an image, and so cannot be edited within a word processor unless it is first passed through an Optical Character Recognition (OCR) program. Also note that because faxes are sent as graphical images, it would be significantly quicker and cheaper to send straightforward textual messages as e-mail rather than as faxes.

Data services

The most common use for a data service is e-mail and, where practicable, access to Internet sites. However, it can also be used from on board to remotely log in to an office computer system, or to allow remote maintenance of the boat's computer systems.

The key point here is the data rate (or speed) of the connection. A typical land phone line and modem will run at around 28.8 kbps (kilobits per second), or an ISDN line at 64 kbps. Apart from the much more expensive INMARSAT B service with high speed data (HSD), you will be running at 9.6 kbps or less when connecting to data services over a cellphone, and 2.4 kbps over Mini-M.

Data access is identical to using a modem on your home PC, with standard packages such as *Microsoft Outlook* for e-mail, *Internet Explorer* for web access, or *PC Anywhere* for remote control of PC systems. For Internet access, you will also need an Internet service provider (ISP). It is worth considering one that has local access points in all of the countries you intend to visit, as this allows you to make a local call rather than an international one. Also, avoid those ISPs who provide an excessively friendly front end overloaded with sound effects, speech output and animations, as these seldom work reliably over a slow communications link – for example, CompuServe no longer support the use of their service over mobile phones.

We can expect to see an increasing number of specialist data services arising in the near future, offering additional facilities. These may include weather and navigation information, re-routeing your messages to alternative e-mail addresses or resending e-mails as fax messages or normal post, and other related services.

Mobile phones (cellphones)

Many yachtsmen will be familiar with the GSM cellphone. GSM stands for Global System for Mobile Telecommunications and is a cellular digital radio technology which has been adopted pretty much worldwide. A GSM cellphone can send and receive fax and e-mail messages as well as the more normal voice communications.

Mayday!

Since the first Mayday message in the days of the *RMS Titanic*, maritime distress and safety communications have been achieved by shore stations or other vessels maintaining a listening watch and relaying safety messages to rescue authorities over specific HF, MF and VHF radio channels. General communications or 'public correspondence' have also been achieved by linking these radio systems onto the public telephone network via shore stations.

Since the Global Maritime Distress and Safety System (GMDSS) was introduced in early 1999, many vessels and coast radio stations are no longer obliged to keep a listening watch on the old safety channels. Instead Mayday and safety messages are handled automatically by the GMDSS, using special Digital Selective Calling (DSC) channels operating over VHF, MF, HF radio and satellite communications systems.

Before the GMDSS was introduced, yachtsmen were quick to discover that their cellular mobile phones (cellphones) offered cheaper and more convenient communications with those ashore than using 'link calls' to shore radio stations. Some yachtsmen ventured to sea without VHF radios and inevitably cellphones were used to summon emergency services. With cheap global communications systems becoming available it is obvious that the temptation will be to ignore the official GMDSS system and to rely on other systems.

The authors stress that although using non-official communications systems to summon help *might* work, it cannot be guaranteed to do so. Therefore, whether required to by the GMDSS or not, ALL vessels should be fitted with GMDSS communications equipment appropriate to the area they will be operating in, in addition to any commercial communications system they may desire.

For the coastal sailor, a cellphone is ideal. In many sailing areas it will work up to about 10 miles offshore, and it offers fax and data services as well as voice, all in a compact and low cost unit. For coastal use a normal hand-held phone works reasonably well. However, range can be improved by installing a cellular antenna at the masthead, connected to a car-type phone handset at the chart table. The best option though, is to use a high-power unit such as the Motorola 2700, which transmits 8W of power as opposed to the 2W of a hand-held unit. This gives significantly better range.

In most of Europe cellphones use the GSM standard, and both Cellnet and Vodaphone can be used throughout Europe (One to One and others work on a different frequency, and use outside the UK is much more limited unless a dual frequency handset is used). However, outside Europe there are a number of alternative cellphone standards, and although some dual USA/Europe cellphones are on the market it may be easier to rent a cellphone in non-GSM areas. Some of these are still analogue services, for example in the USA, and achieving reliable fax and data links with these is not easy.

For fax and data use, the cellphone needs to connect to a PC. Usually a 'PC Card' (see chapter 9) connection is best, as it leaves the PC's serial port free for other purposes. PC Cards tend to be more reliable than infra-red connections on board. You will also need to have fax and data enabled on your airtime contract, and you will get separate phone numbers for these services.

INMARSAT Mini-M

This service has revolutionised communications offshore, giving voice, fax and data services over most ocean areas at a low cost and with a compact antenna system (typically 45 to 75 centimetres diameter). Mini-M systems are marketed under a number of names such as BoatPhone or Tracphone.

As stated, Mini-M offers voice communications and also fax and data, though the latter two only operate at a modest 2.4 kbps. For fax, this is a quarter of the speed that a land line fax runs at, and less than a tenth of the speed of a land data line.

The combination of a slow data rate and the time delays from the satellite link means that not all fax machines work reliably with this service – it is advisable to obtain a list of approved models that work, to install both on the boat and at the shoreside. Similarly, if you are doing your faxing from a PC, it's recommended to use a

*INMARSAT's
Mini-M system
offers voice, fax
and data
transmissions
using spot beam
technology*

package such as *Enigma*, which has been designed to work with Mini-M systems. In the authors' experience, general purpose products such as *Microsoft Fax* and some of the lower cost fax/data modems do not work well with Mini-M systems.

Note that Mini-M systems have a built-in modem for data access, but just a standard phone socket for fax. So to have both fax and data on your PC, you must connect a serial port on the PC to the data port on the Mini-M (for data), and also a separate modem on the PC to connect to the fax socket on the Mini-M (for fax).

At the time of writing there is a new service in the pipeline called Global Area Network (GAN), based on INMARSAT's M4 development programme. This offers 64 kbit/sec (many times the data rate of Mini-M), and although it will initially just be for land users, no doubt in time we shall also see this adopted by the marine market.

INMARSAT B   This is a much more powerful INMARSAT system, usually installed on larger vessels. It has largely replaced the older INMARSAT A system for new vessel installations. Using a 1 metre diameter stabilised antenna, it offers full worldwide coverage (except for the polar regions, which are inaccessible to geostationary satellite systems such as INMARSAT).

Services include voice and fax, and data running at 9.6 kbps. There is also a high speed data option that runs at 64 kbps, the same rate as an ISDN line, which is ideal for sending and receiving large amounts of data or for fast Internet access, as well as for tasks such as video conferencing. To make this powerful satellite communications system run at its full potential, third-party PC software and hardware should be used to increase throughput.

Future systems

At the time of writing there is a whole range of satellite services in the final stages of technical implementation, most not yet commercially launched. These include Globalstar, ICO, Teledesic and VSAT and are really aimed at commercial marine users with high volumes of traffic. These services will offer high data throughput often at fixed cost. Multiple 64 kbit/sec lines can be used for voice, fax or data communications. It is unlikely that these services will be aimed directly at the marine leisure user, however, as with most technological advances in commercial marine technologies, the leisure user is sure to benefit to some extent.

Messaging systems

Unlike phone-based systems, messaging systems are designed for the transfer of plain text; a little bit like the old telex network, they do not offer voice or fax services.

However, some programs such as *WordSat* exert a bit of ingenuity by encoding non-text computer files into text in a form that is

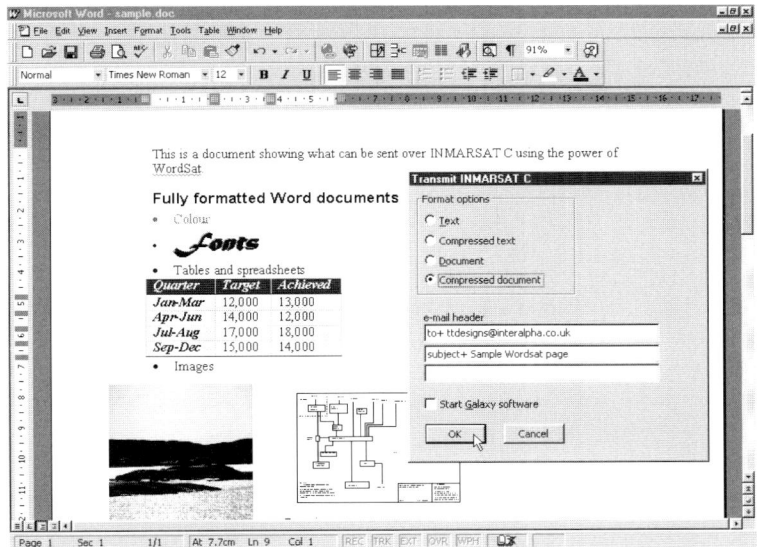

Even with plain text messaging systems, it is possible to send rich, graphical documents, albeit slowly

suitable to go over the network. This gives the user two main benefits when sending to another *WordSat* user (whether ashore or afloat): first, he can compress his messages, which can reduce the communications bill; and secondly, he can send binary data such as formatted word processor documents, spreadsheets and images.

INMARSAT C   This was the first of the INMARSAT systems to be launched, and is ideal for marine users who do not need voice communications, and don't wish to transmit large amounts of data. In addition to ordinary messages, INMARSAT C can also be used for receiving NAVTEX and for sending distress signals through the GMDSS. INMARSAT C can also be used to poll the position of an equipped vessel from ashore at relatively low cost.

Complete INMARSAT C system. Trimble's 'Galaxy' terminal software runs well on a standard PC

Outgoing messages are prepared, and incoming messages read, on a dedicated terminal or on a PC using software supplied with the system. This software interfaces through the PC's serial port to the INMARSAT C transceiver, which connects via a coaxial cable to a compact omni-directional antenna.

When sending messages, you can designate whether they are to be sent as fax or e-mail to the recipient. In the UK and many other countries, people can send messages to an INMARSAT C system by phoning or faxing the maritime section of their telephone company, and having the cost of the message added to their bill.

To send e-mail to the boat, a mailbox needs to be set up with British Telecom's C-Club or a similar service. This enables the boat owner to restrict who can send e-mail to the boat, which is important since they pick up the cost of this traffic!

INMARSAT C is a store and forward system, so messages destined for your boat are stored if your system is not switched on, for forwarding when you do switch on. Similarly, on the boat the receiver stores messages until they are downloaded to your PC.

At present the software provided with INMARSAT C hardware is still DOS based (*Capsat* or *Galaxy*), to meet the requirements of commercial shipping and the GMDSS. However, products such as *WordSat* allow messages to be sent from and received into *Microsoft Word* without having to run the DOS software.

Radio telex

In the marine area, MF/HF radio is steadily being replaced by satellite communications. Morse was discontinued in 1998, and British Telecom plans to discontinue radio link calls in 2001. However, MF/HF radio telex is being maintained as part of the GMDSS system, partly because of the large installed user base, and partly because of the limitations of geostationary satellites in very high latitudes.

Radio telex allows telex and, through an appropriate gateway, e-mail to be sent and received. A special radio modem is used between the PC and the radio, and data travels at a very slow 50 bits per second. There are a number of commercial services available, but transmission costs are higher than for INMARSAT C, so unless an MF/HF transceiver is already installed, or is required for other purposes, this would not be a recommended system nowadays.

As well as commercial services, ham radio enthusiasts have developed a similar range of services, but which can be used at no charge. In order to take advantage of these kinds of services, you will need to have an amateur radio set and licence, as opposed to a marine radio licence.

New generation MF/HF data services

As mentioned above, commercial radio telex provision by national telephone carriers is now effectively defunct. A number of new services have grown from ham radio usage to fill the gap, offering a similar range of services to those that the national telcos used to offer. As such, HF radio e-mail may be suitable for those going blue-water cruising. Two operators in the field are PinOak Digital and Globe Wireless, both American. Globe Wireless's service offers upwards of sixteen ground stations and provides ship-management and fleet tracking services to commercial operators, as well as e-mail and file transfer facilities. PinOak Digital probably offers the service most appropriate to leisure yachtsmen.

Data rates are very slow, suitable only for e-mail. Communication can also be unreliable due to radio propagation issues, signal fading, interference, and stronger transmitters going over the top of your own. In spite of these limitations, if you have an SSB radio on board for general marine communication or weatherfax reception and do not wish to fit a satellite communications system or take a ham radio licence, this system does offer a relatively low cost worldwide messaging system.

Signing up to these services requires payment of a registration fee, which includes a proprietary modem that is connected to the PC's serial port. There is then an annual fee as well as a fee based on the amount of data sent.

Orbcomm

Orbcomm is one of the new generation of low earth orbit communication service providers. They operate satellites and ground earth stations (GES) which allow e-mail messaging from and to anywhere on the earth's surface. As well as e-mail messages, termed GlobalGrams, the system offers other services such as *OrbWeather* – short text forecasts based on your current position.

Hand-held receivers, such as Magellan's GSC 100, incorporate a small screen, command buttons and a numeric keypad for composing messages. Software is available that allows message handling and some control of the GSC 100 by a PC connected via a serial port.

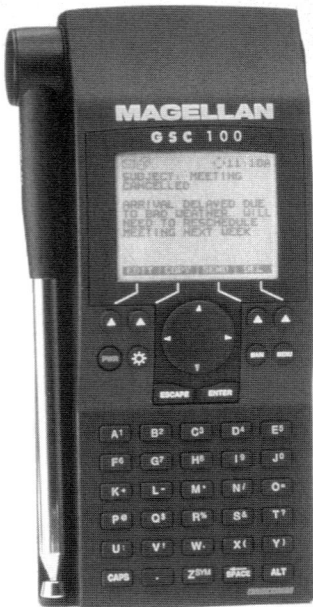

There are many sources of weather information available to the yachtsman, but access to them is dependent upon the communications equipment on board. Unless indicated otherwise, this information is available free of charge.

Weatherfax

Weatherfax consists of synoptic (current weather) and forecast maps produced by meteorologists, covering information such as pressure, wind, weather, sea state and currents, and even icing. There is extensive coverage of Northern Europe, North America and the Caribbean, with maps transmitted regularly over HF radio. As well as being receivable on a dedicated weatherfax receiver, they can be received on an SSB radio interfaced to a PC that is equipped with suitable software.

Although it can take some experience to successfully receive and interpret weatherfax images, this is a very low cost way of adding a high-quality meteorological facility to your on board PC system. With practice, mariners should be able to get a better understanding of current and impending weather than would be possible with

Typical weatherfax images that may be received using a SSB radio connected to a PC

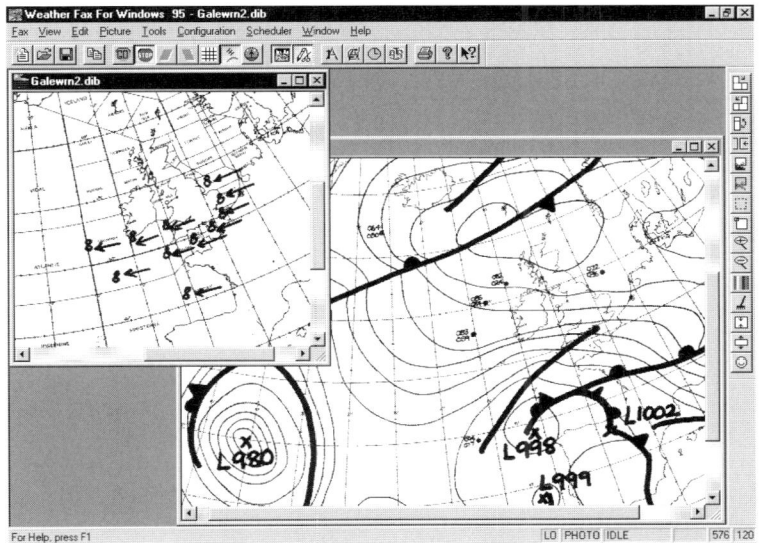

other methods on their own. Particularly when interpreted together with other forecast information (spoken forecasts and shore station reports, NAVTEX etc), weatherfaxes can be very useful indeed.

A simple weatherfax package will typically come supplied with a 'demodulator' that connects the audio output port of the radio to the PC's serial port. With these basic, low cost systems, scheduling and tuning of the radio is left to the user, but they are capable of surprisingly high-quality results.

More sophisticated systems are able to control suitable radios (eg the ICOM PCR-1000 and the Lowe HF-150) and may be set up to automatically tune the radio in to a suitable schedule of frequencies (using a serial connection to the PC's COM port) and use the PC's line-in connector on the sound card to obtain even higher quality images.

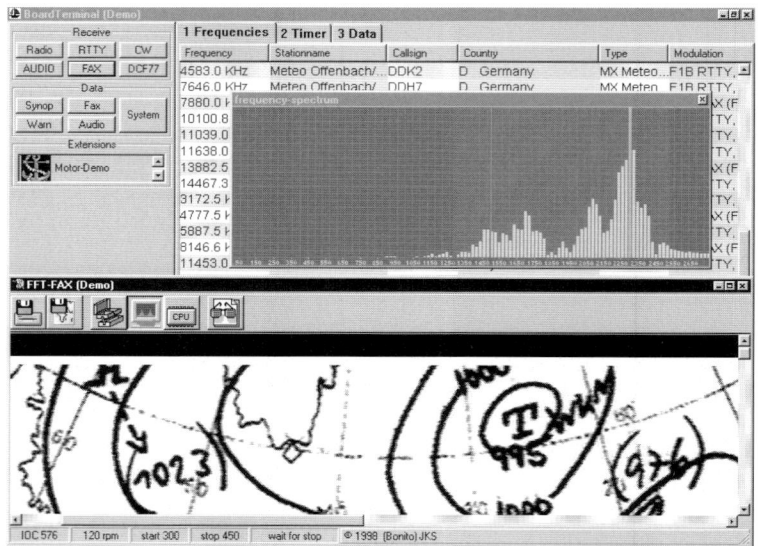

With radio control, scheduling, tuning scopes and image enhancement tools, some systems offer the user powerful control of weatherfax receipt

Weatherfax is a very useful weather resource for yachtsmen and should be available free of charge for the near future. You only need an SSB receiver and suitable antenna to receive weatherfax, not a complete SSB transceiver, so the equipment is not expensive. Do bear in mind that the information you receive using weatherfax is not generally designed for the layman, and to get the most out of received charts you may need to study a suitable guide.

The same data may be available in a number of other ways, for example the UK Meteorological Office currently puts some of the weatherfax data that it transmits over HF up on its web site, and also offers a faxback service (using a premium rate phone line).

From a European perspective, the best weatherfax transmissions are currently from Hamburg (formerly Offenbach) with the Meteorological Office at Bracknell and the Navy at Northwood being nearly as good if not quite as reliable. The stations tend to transmit images simultaneously on different frequencies, so it is usually possible to get good pictures in spite of adverse atmospherics.

For new users and for those who have tried and discounted weatherfax because they have been unable to receive suitable quality images, consider the following, which may help.

◆ Your greatest enemies are poor antenna installation (and grounding) and electrical interference. If you experience interference while listening to programmes on other frequencies, you will have trouble receiving weatherfax. Solution: identify the source of the interference and switch it off! RF (radio frequency) energy behaves differently from DC electricity – even those with good knowledge of the latter may require some help with the former.

◆ When tuning, remember to tune the radio *down* for USB transmissions and *up* for LSB ones. Judge when it looks right on screen rather than blindly sticking to the nominal 1.9kHz amount.

◆ Hearing the signal is very important to successful tuning – if your radio switches off its speakers when you plug in the demodulator, try adding a 'Y' connector and a separate speaker. Experienced operators can hear when the signal is 'right'.

◆ There are many controls on the average radio receiver. Change only one thing at a time and wait for it to settle down. If it makes no difference, change it back before changing anything else or you'll get lost.

◆ Very few people get it right first time – be prepared to spend some time perfecting your skills. Long winter evenings are ideal, and with a PC you won't be wasting paper and ink.

It can also be challenging identifying which transmissions should be listened out for. Whilst each station usually transmits its own schedule of broadcasts at frequent intervals, for the new user, up-to-date details of transmission schedules are contained within the UK Hydrographic Office's *Admiralty List of Radio Signals, vol 3*. There are also several private publications offering listings, and the Internet is a good source of this type of information.

Synoptic reports

As part of the data sharing agreements of the WMO (World Meteorological Organisation), current weather (synoptic) reports are transmitted over SSB radio in an encoded text format called SYNOP. The data is sent in groups of five characters, and the traditional way of decoding this was to look up each set of characters in a code book, and transcribe it to text. However, modern weather packages will not only receive the data, but also decode it and display weather reports at each station. Some can even interpolate the data to draw a weather map.

SYNOP data sent consists of current values (as well as trends) for air pressure, wind speed and direction, sea state, air and sea temperature, cloud cover, precipitation and much more, typically updated every 6 or 12 hours.

If you receive SYNOP information regularly, some weather software allows you to create animated sequences from stored data – this can be very useful in anticipating future weather.

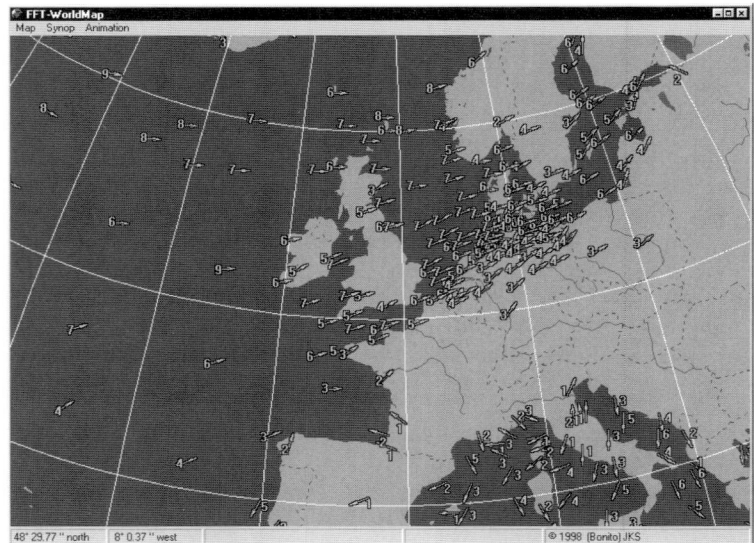

Viewing historical sequences of synoptic (current) data can be nearly as informative as studying professional forecasts in helping to predict the weather

NAVTEX

NAVTEX is primarily a navigational information service that also carries some weather forecast information, particularly severe weather warnings. It is transmitted on a fixed frequency of 518kHz, and on INMARSAT C, with the seas and oceans divided into a number of specific regions. These English language radio transmissions are broadcast every four hours, with a nominal range of 200–300 nautical miles, and they can be received with a dedicated NAVTEX receiver.

As part of the Global Maritime Distress and Safety System (GMDSS), NAVTEX is a free and reliable source of weather information, with improving coverage and talk of enhancing the weather information available.

Yachtsmen who already have a PC and an SSB receiver or an INMARSAT C transceiver on board may, with the addition of simple software, receive these broadcasts on their PC. In fact, most weatherfax software has the ability to receive NAVTEX messages.

Although using your PC is a good way of receiving NAVTEX broadcasts, the system is really designed for unattended operation using a dedicated receiver unit. Using the PC, however, gives you a useful and flexible independent back-up at low cost; another advantage is the ability to store old messages on disk for later review.

Choosing an SSB radio

If you have, or are planning to have, an SSB transceiver on board for general communications or for MF/HF e-mail, it is more than likely to have been professionally installed and connected to an insulated backstay aerial. This set-up is ideal for receiving weather data, time broadcasts and long distance spoken communications.

Whilst a much lower cost SSB receiver may be used to receive the same broadcasts, it is worth bearing in mind that with radios you get what you pay for. So start with the best SSB receiver you can afford, opting for a good-quality basic receiver rather than a lower-quality receiver with dozens of unnecessary controls and functions.

A basic receiver should offer single side band (SSB) as well as amplitude modulation (AM) and Morse code (CW) modes. It should tune between 100kHz and 30mHz with a tuning accuracy (especially at lower frequencies) of 100Hz or less. As well as an audio headphone output (which can be used for basic weatherfax demodulators), it should have a line-out connector for use with the more modern PC sound card-based PC weather systems. A direct 12VDC or 24VDC feed avoids troublesome electrical interference which is often experienced when running these radios through a transformer.

Equally important is a good antenna installation. As already stated, the best is an insulated backstay, but good-quality active antennas may also give perfectly acceptable results. The antenna installation (and the radio itself) should be appropriately grounded and connected using marine-grade coaxial cable of the correct impedance, using sympathetic cable routeing and purpose-made watertight cable glands where necessary.

Some PC-based radio weather receiver systems are able to control suitable SSB receivers. This is a boon as it allows you to use the PC software to set up receiving schedules, whereupon it can automatically re-tune the radio at predefined times. With a bit of experience, it is possible to use such a set-up for completely unattended receipt of weatherfax, SYNOP and NAVTEX broadcasts.

Weather satellite images

Weatherfax is a great source of current and forecast weather reports, but there are many parts of the world where it is not available, and this is where weather satellite systems come into their own. A weather satellite system is usually supplied as a complete package of antenna, receiver and software. Operation is easier than weatherfax because the software predicts when the satellites are transmitting, automatically tunes in the receiver and receives the transmitted images for you, totally unattended. The receiver can be mounted at deck level, but should be kept clear of sources of electrical and radio interference as the satellite transmission power is very low, only 5W, transmitted from about 600 miles away.

Whilst all of the sources of weather information discussed so far provide weather data that has been prepared by meteorologists, weather satellite images provide raw weather information. This means that there is no time lag in its preparation, so it is always much more up-to-date than other sources. The downside is that you need to do all the analysis yourself, so to get the most from these systems, you should have at least a passing acquaintance with meteorological practices.

All boats can receive polar satellite images, known as Wefax, which are on a North–South circumpolar orbit, with each orbit taking about 100 minutes. In mid latitudes they typically pass overhead three or four times a day, but at higher latitudes the passes become more frequent as the satellites converge towards the poles. The satellite takes a continuous photograph of the patch of earth beneath it, simultaneously transmitting it down to any receivers under its path. You receive a rectangular strip aligned approximately N–S, and the higher the satellite rises above your horizon the greater the area covered.

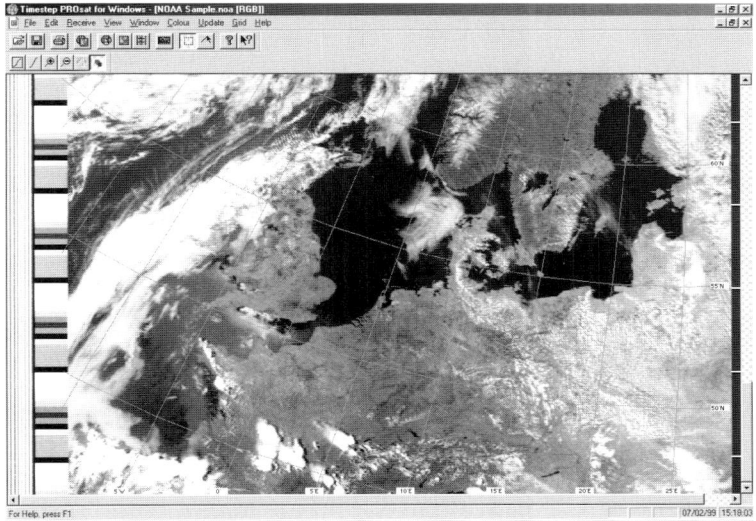

Composite image of NW Europe created from NOAA weather images (visible and infra-red)

In fact it is actually taking two photographs – one with visible light and the other infra-red (both as grey scale images). The visible light image is great for showing the textures of the top of the cloud, through the shadows cast, and also for picking up patches of sea fog which do not show up on the infra-red images, but they are only available during the day. Infra-red images effectively measure temperature, so they are available at all times. If there is cloud, they pick up the temperature of the top of the cloud – and the colder it is, the higher the cloud top is. When there is no cloud it picks up the sea or land temperature, which can show thermal currents such as the Gulf Stream, and also pick up icing. The weather satellite software can then add coastlines and a grid to these images (very useful when there is extensive cloud cover), and also combine them into a realistically coloured image that combines the information held in each individual image.

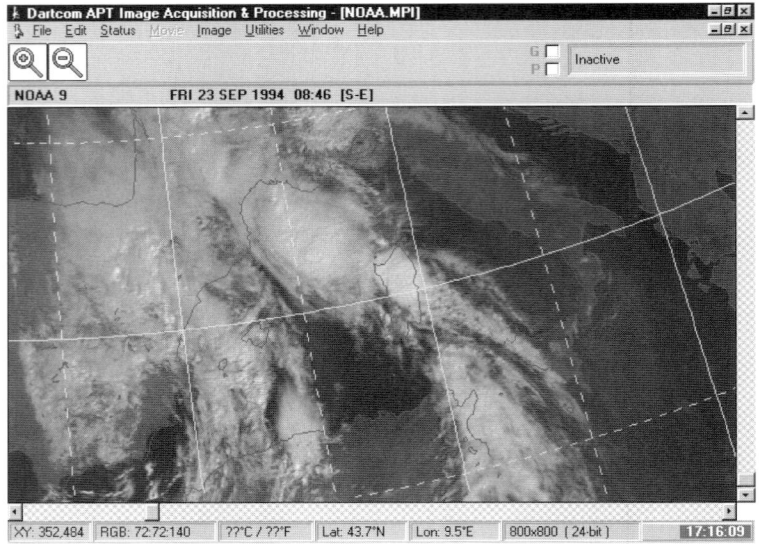

*NOAA image of
the western
Mediterranean,
with land outlines
and a lat/long
grid overlaid to
aid interpretation*

Boats large enough to have a stabilised dish antenna installed can also track geostationary satellites 'parked' over the equator – a dish antenna is required because these satellites are at a very high altitude, producing a very weak signal. Because of their altitude, geostationary satellites can see the whole hemisphere (which it divides up into smaller sections), so the area of weather that can be seen is much greater than with orbiting satellites. Images are transmitted at regular intervals of about 30 minutes, which enables very vivid animations to be created. These can be viewed directly on the PC, or transmitted onto the boat's TV system.

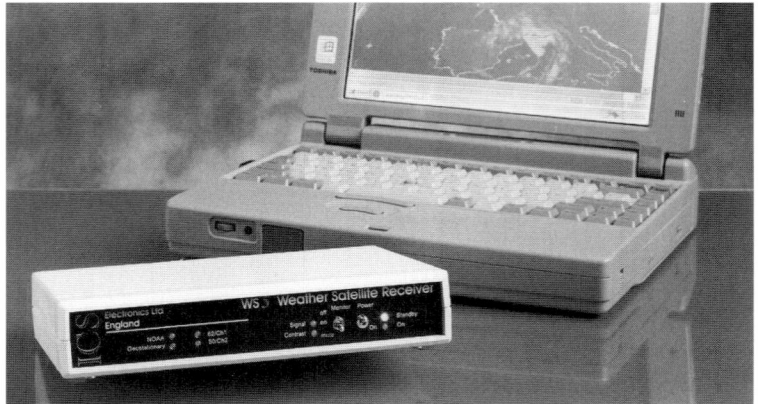

*A small decoder,
attached to an
antenna is all that
is required, in
addition to a
standard PC*

6 • Vessel Administration

Vessel administration programs can cover a wide range of facilities, but they all have one thing in common: to make the running of the vessel easier. This can include managing the boat's documentation, tracking expenses (and also income for charter boats), monitoring the boat's systems and scheduling and tracking maintenance work.

The usefulness of these programs is not confined to the complex and sophisticated systems to be found on board superyachts – as smaller pleasure yachts get increasingly complex and include more and more systems, it can be extremely challenging for the skipper of a small boat to keep a handle on all the important aspects of running the boat.

Documentation To begin at the beginning, with the development of a new boat, a package such as *Techman* will let all those involved in the project – designer, boatyard, project manager and owner – track the whole process, beginning with the initial specification, obtaining costings and quotations, through the entire build process. At the end of the day this provides the owner with a complete 'as built' specification and set of drawings. This set of documents can be used as the basis for planning any future work on board the vessel. Although it can be a considerable effort to enter all of the data into the PC, if this is carried out through the build process (as is necessary to track the project anyway) it should not be too onerous a task.

Carrying on from here, when a boat is handed over to the owner it comes with a huge pile of manuals, drawings and specifications covering everything from light fittings to the generator. On a larger yacht this can easily run to several bookshelves of documentation, and it can be a nightmare to find the right manual. In time, we are bound to see more of this documentation provided on CD-ROM or DVD, either in HTML format so it can be viewed with any web browser, or in a custom document viewing package.

Boat management When it comes to actually running the boat, there are a number of boat management packages to help with this. These all offer similar functionality, but some have a better user interface than others, and some can be configured to suit the user's specific needs whereas with others everything in the program is fixed.

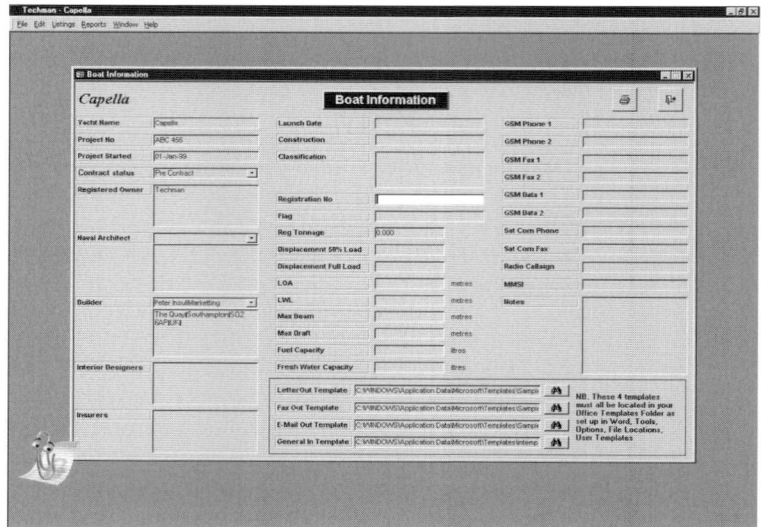

Large amounts of information associated with the building of a boat may be stored for the owner in an on board system

Perhaps the most useful aspect of these programs lies in their ability to schedule and track maintenance and other work carried out on the boat, and in association with these to keep track of equipment and stores on the boat. Enter the periodic maintenance requirements of your equipment, and the program will produce work lists of all scheduled maintenance work, which can be assigned to different crew members or contractors, and ticked off when completed. The locations of equipment and spares can be stored, as well as the quantity of items held on board. The contacts list can keep track of all suppliers, crew members and others, and a cash accounting facility allows the boat's expenses to be tracked, with some programs offering multi-currency facilities.

Passage planning and log book facilities are also incorporated into many programs, though the log keeping is not comparable with the facilities to be found in a dedicated chart plotter. However, the passage planning facilities can be useful, including the ability to create crew and equipment lists, to predict passage times and fuel consumption, and to create stores lists based on the passage time and number of crew carried.

Systems monitoring

So far we have just looked at manual systems, where a crew member is responsible for entering information into the system. The next stage, extensively used on larger yachts, is to use a PC-based systems monitoring package. Sensors pass information to the PC about different parts of the vessel: the engines, generators, hydraulics and tankage etc, right through to the fridge temperature, portholes, navigation lights and security systems. Monitoring these devices on the PC offers a number of significant advantages over traditional displays and alarms.

First, as well as simply displaying current readings, the logged data can be used to spot trends to give warning of possible problems or help to diagnose faults. Secondly, the software in the PC can interlink different sensors to give better monitoring facilities than are available with stand-alone systems; this is especially the case on larger vessels with more complex systems. This can also be extended by combining monitoring systems and maintenance scheduling into an integrated system, so that equipment maintenance can be triggered, based on actual usage levels. Finally, by integrating the monitoring system with the rest of the computer systems, space can be saved and installation costs reduced, as well as allowing the system to be monitored from any PC on the boat's network.

As well as monitoring data from on board sensors, some more sophisticated systems will also provide control of remotely sited actuators. This control can be effected by a crew member responding to sensor data shown on the PC, or automatically by the PC system itself, according to tolerances and thresholds programmed-in by the user.

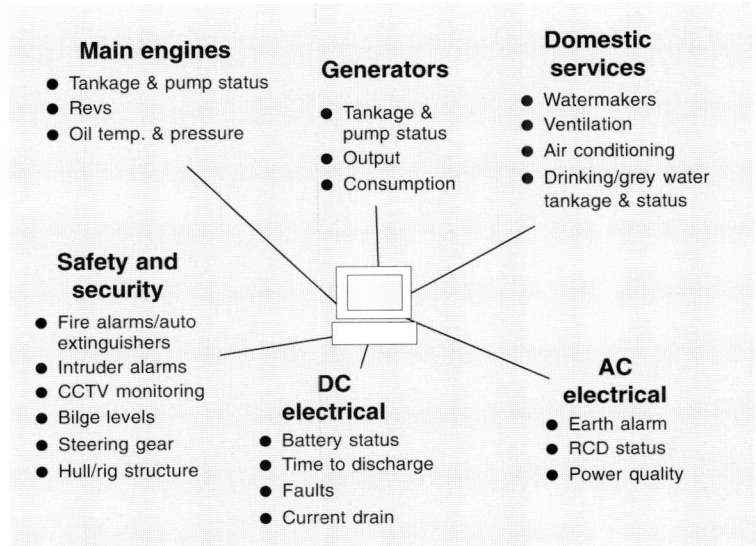

Sophisticated monitoring systems will become commonplace on smaller yachts in the future

Main engines
- Tankage & pump status
- Revs
- Oil temp. & pressure

Generators
- Tankage & pump status
- Output
- Consumption

Domestic services
- Watermakers
- Ventilation
- Air conditioning
- Drinking/grey water tankage & status

Safety and security
- Fire alarms/auto extinguishers
- Intruder alarms
- CCTV monitoring
- Bilge levels
- Steering gear
- Hull/rig structure

DC electrical
- Battery status
- Time to discharge
- Faults
- Current drain

AC electrical
- Earth alarm
- RCD status
- Power quality

Whilst the vessel management capabilities of an on board PC system may not be as exciting as chart plotting, communications or weather, they can make boat management a much easier process, particularly as the systems on board become more complex.

Video monitoring

With a suitable interface card in the PC, the computer can be used to drive video cameras which may be used to monitor the engines, to monitor blind spots or allow the sails to be checked from down below, or as a security system. A more complex system will allow multiple cameras to be monitored at the same time, and cameras to be triggered by other sensors, such as a heat sensor in the engine room or a motion detector on deck. Also, once the video imagery is in the computer, it can easily be made available across the network, or even remotely to a shore station.

There are a number of options with cameras. Colour is obviously available, but mono or infra-red cameras operate much better in low light levels or at night. Also some cameras offer the facility to have a remotely operated pan and tilt or zoom function, which can be controlled from the PC.

Though this may seem like the realm of science fiction, small video cameras are surprisingly inexpensive nowadays. With their small size and low power consumption, they are ideally suited to 'keeping an eye' on those areas of a vessel that may be hazardous or impracticable to check regularly.

The PC is an ideal appliance to gather all this information together and to display it conveniently in the navigation station, so although these systems are presently confined to larger yachts, as costs fall, they should soon be found on board a typical leisure yacht.

7 • Training and Entertainment

Having examined the wealth of marine software now available, we have seen how using a PC on board can help you get more out of your sailing while planning passages and actually under way. It does not stop there, however, because the 'multimedia' capabilities of newer computers are ideally suited to delivering high-quality educational and entertainment material.

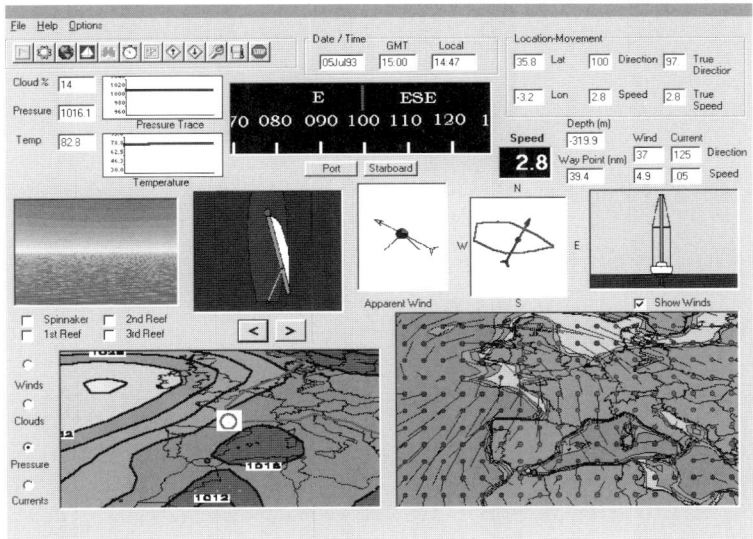

Comprehensive modelling of many variables can make these systems realistic, which aids understanding

Learning can be enjoyable!

As well as excellent programs to help you learn new skills (or at least the theory) during long winter evenings when the boat is laid up, there are also many training programs that can help you brush up your skills during the season.

Taking on board the maxim that 'to be effective, learning must be fun', software manufacturers have written training packages that are not only educational, but enjoyable to use as well. It is not uncommon to see and hear full colour video simulations, along with log books and course material structured so you can learn at your own pace.

And if such 'edutainment' weren't enough, the PC is an ideal platform for playing purely recreational games and, increasingly, for viewing full-length feature films. This is great for keeping bored children occupied or for those times when the row to the Happy Yottie across a rainy anchorage just doesn't appeal!

Training software may be split broadly into simulators and tutors; whilst some simulators offer self-test facilities, tutors nearly always include some element of simulation as well.

Simulators

Often at sea there are many things going on at once. The sailor may not have the luxury of time to evaluate the cause and effect of his actions in isolation from external factors. Simulator programs are an attempt to do just that, to take one aspect of the navigator's craft and to allow him to practise it in controlled conditions to increase his skills.

Because real world factors are modelled in the program, users are presented with a fairly lifelike representation of what they might experience at sea – without the mêlée of wind, tide, boat, crew, visibility etc which often serve to hinder the learning process.

Thus the user can practise such skills as the recognition of lights, buoyage, sound signals, even Morse code. The idea is that if the simulation is realistic enough, is repeated often enough and is not too predictable, then the skill becomes second nature.

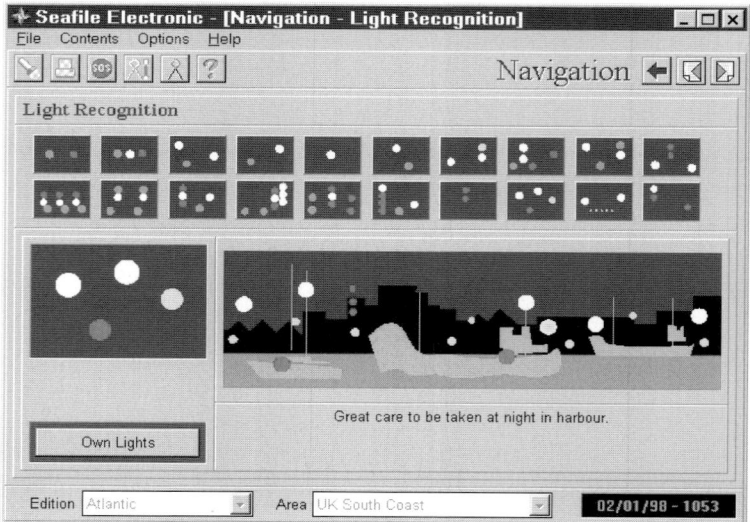

One of the best uses for training software is in navigation light recognition

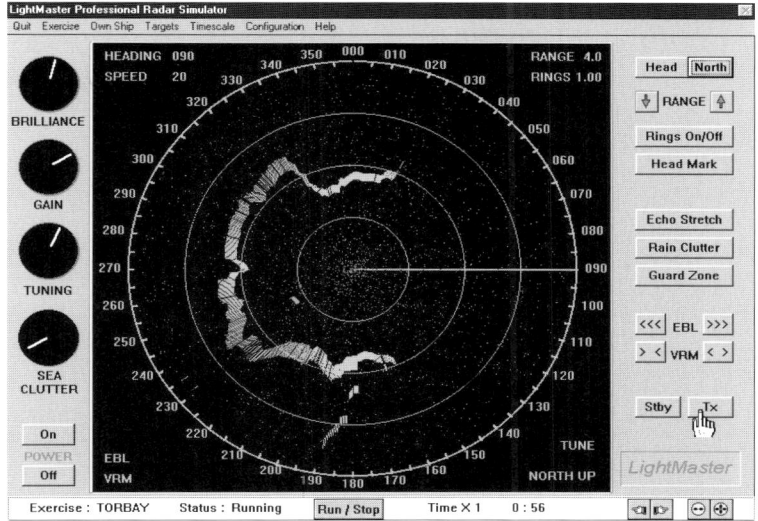

*Simulators help
yachtsmen master
many complicated
controls to get
the best out of a
radar set*

Simulators are ideal for more complex learning situations based around modern technology – for the occasional yachtsmen, coping with the range of functions available on modern radars and DSC radios can be challenging. Relying on such equipment without full knowledge of its operational behaviour could well be dangerous – bad decisions can be made due to misinterpretation of information that the equipment supplies.

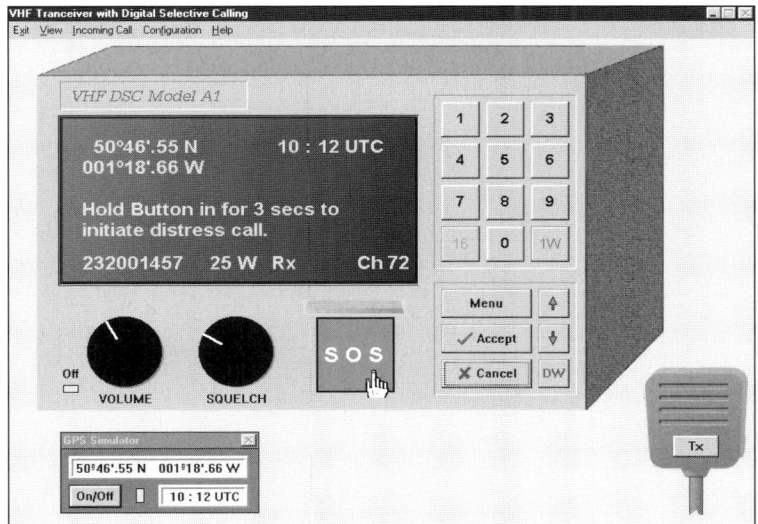

*A DSC Simulator
enables a
yachtsman to
practise for
distress situations
without the risk of
sending a false
GMDSS alert*

Radar simulators teach you how the various controls affect the clarity of the received image. Again, the simulator models various environmental conditions (rain, waves etc) and their effect on the image may be seen, this instant feedback aiding the learning process.

The introduction of the GMDSS means that more and more yachtsmen are fitting VHF Digital Selective Calling (DSC) radios on board. Whilst DSC automates many traditionally spoken radio tasks, such as calling up other vessels or initiating distress calls, the change in method has been challenging for many. A DSC simulator lets you practise using a typical set, without the worry of initiating a false distress alert on a 'live' DSC radio.

Simulators generally have fairly low computer requirements and do not require connections to external equipment.

Tutors

Where simulators excel is in aiding recognition; however, they are seldom suitable as aids to actual understanding of topics. This is where tutors come in. Tutors tend to take full advantage of the PC's multimedia capabilities, offering structured learning courses for the beginner right through to the experienced mariner. Tutor programs are available which cover navigation, seamanship, meteorology, even the collision regulations.

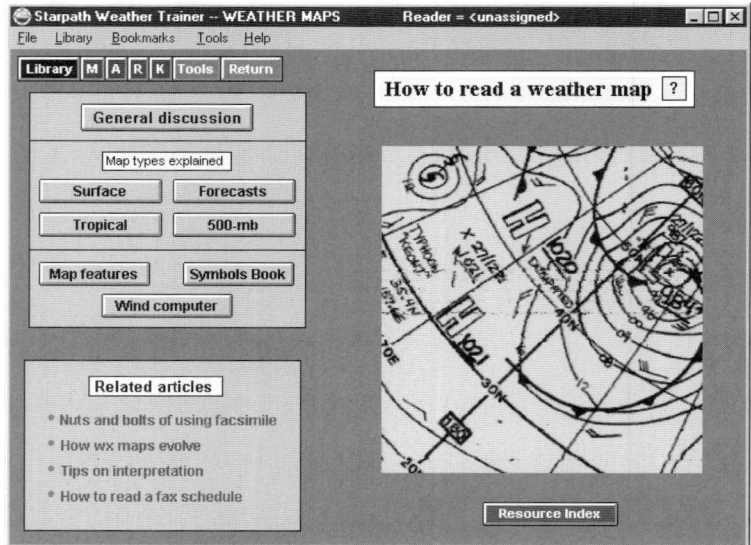

Tutors come in all shapes and sizes and, if well designed, can really help in understanding a new topic

Most programs are organised into a series of instructional 'chapters', each covering a particular topic and linked together with reference material. Often they will have extensive glossaries, with pictures, and even sound and video footage, to aid your understanding. Many programs boast a log book, where you can record your progress through the system, as well as question and answer sections to measure your understanding of the material.

As with printed educational material, the usefulness of a particular program to any individual student varies enormously and is a very personal thing. For this reason, you should take the opportunity of trying out this kind of software before purchase, if at all possible.

Many yachting magazines review computer training packages in their book pages and may be able to advise you; but better still, avoid the classified advertisements and visit a marine computing specialist where you may be able to try before you buy.

Games

The worldwide computer games industry is massive and growing very quickly – high-quality interactive multimedia presentation of action, arcade and more intellectual gameplay is a compelling combination, whether played to help unwind after a busy day at work, or simply as an alternative to more passive televisual entertainment.

On board, the same is true and computer games can certainly help while away long hours on passage. But games are quite demanding upon a PC, with heavy use of graphics. If you rely on your PC

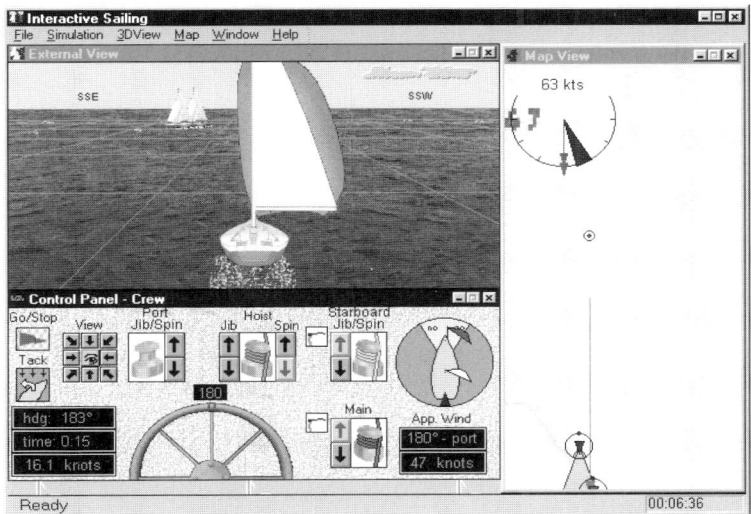

With sound and video capability, educational programs can be surprisingly realistic

for critical navigation tasks, bear in mind that some of the 'big name' resource hungry games can cause problems with the machine's configuration, causing other programs to stop working properly.

If you insist on using such games software on your boat's PC, install it and thoroughly check that it has not had an adverse effect on your other programs well before you go to sea – although it's unlikely that such a game will actually damage your PC permanently, it may be necessary to reinstall and reconfigure all your 'proper' software from scratch if you experience a problem.

That said, most games are pretty well behaved, particularly ones aimed at the yachting market. Similar to educational simulator programs, the current crop of games have far more options and better graphics than their 'serious' cousins. There are games available that let you take the helm of cruising and racing yachts and powerboats, with realistic scenery, even computer controlled 'virtual opponents' to compete against.

TV and video   Although one would not currently associate TV and video on board with PCs, this will undoubtedly change in the very near future. As the price of high resolution flat screen TFT panels continues to plummet, they will look increasingly attractive as replacements for CRT-based TV sets (as well as falling prices, they will be in demand for their low power consumption, small size and ease of panel mounting).

Also, the Digital Versatile Disc (DVD) has now come of age – for the first time, it is possible to have a full-length, full-motion feature film stored on one CD-ROM sized disc. The DVD is set to replace video cassettes as a distribution medium and, being digital, is ideally suited to work with your on board PC. In fact DVD is increasingly fitted as standard to desktop and laptop PCs.

Given that very few yachtsmen use a video recorder to actually record TV programmes on board, it looks likely that over the next few years, DVD (or its successor) will completely replace video cassettes for playback. This is especially so when you consider that the DVD is physically much smaller than a video cassette as well as being much more reliable in the marine environment.

The last few years have seen an explosion in the growth of the Internet and few would deny that this growth will accelerate even faster in the coming years. As this book goes to press, the Internet, or at least some parts of it, are becoming available through digital television services.

So what is this phenomenon, and could it be useful to yachtsmen?

An Internet history primer

In its early years, the Internet was a little bit like the old American Wild West, a 'place' inhabited by computer scientists, enthusiasts and hackers, who delighted in its informality and complexity and in getting around the limitations of the early technology.

For the Internet to grow, this had to change, and change it has; its various parts now dovetail so neatly with current communications/marketing/entertainment media that it has become a compelling technology that is hard to avoid – even if we should want to. Nowadays, the Internet offers worldwide users a simple, low cost and convenient method of communicating (written, audio and visual), learning and trading, even of delivering certain types of products (software and data).

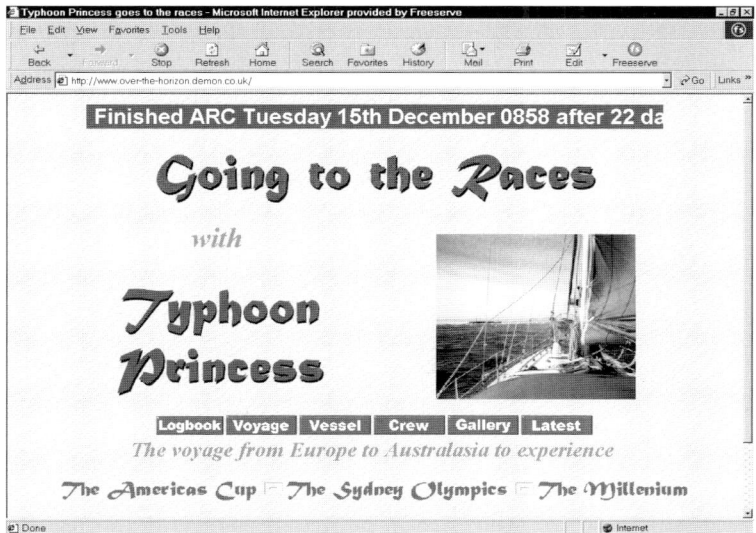

There must be very few yachtsmen who are not aware of the Internet or who have not used the World Wide Web

Internet Basics

The Internet is an informal global network of computers, which are connected together by ordinary telecommunications cables. What makes it special is that the computers all speak the same digital language (or protocol) – TCP/IP – and so can communicate conveniently. The Internet's computers are connected like a spider's web so that there are many different possible pathways from one router to another. TCP/IP takes transmitted data and breaks it down into conveniently sized 'packets' that are then transmitted across the Internet's pathways and reassembled at the other end. Should a packet become damaged in transit (corrupted) or not arrive for any other reason, it will be sent again, often by a different pathway, until all is received and reassembled correctly.

So if a computer should break down, or if a communications link be broken or overloaded with traffic, the 'fault-tolerant' Internet will adapt to make sure that robust communications are nearly always available.

The end-user (that's you) doesn't usually see this behind-the-scenes work – typically, the Internet user is using the Internet through an organisation called an Internet service provider (ISP) whose computers are linked directly to the Internet. Once you've connected to your ISP (often through a phone line), they look after the business of sending and receiving your 'traffic' onto the Internet proper.

It's important to note that the Internet is not owned by anyone. There is not a global organisation that has somehow put the infrastructure in place for the Internet to be. However, it is obviously very costly for such an infrastructure to exist, so who pays for all the computer hardware, cabling and software engineering required?

Ultimately of course, the user pays. This is usually done in one of two ways. Firstly, the end-user pays their ISP a small annual or monthly fee and the ISP pays a much larger fee to the telecommunications company that actually provides the communications service. The second and increasingly common way is for the ISP to provide access free of direct charge to the user; but the ISP gets paid a percentage of each user's telephone charges by the phone company.

Even the telecommunications giants are not large enough to build complete worldwide networks themselves, so they tend to come to arrangements between themselves, whereby they agree to carry each other's traffic on a sort of swap basis. This is very similar to how the original postal and telephone systems developed, and because the telecommunications companies are all using equipment which speaks the same protocol (TCP/IP), the Internet has been able to grow very quickly into a large, powerful and reliable system.

This is all very well for onshore users, using powerful PCs and land-line connections direct to the Internet, but sadly not all of the benefits of the Internet are currently available to today's yachtsmen.

There are, though, some aspects that are incredibly useful for yachtsmen, and taking the time to have a grasp of basic concepts that are often 'hidden' from our shore-bound cousins allows you to get much more from the Internet than you might think.

Internet for yachtsmen

The Internet actually comprises an enormous range of tools and facilities, with strange names like FTP, WWW, Gopher, Telnet, POP3, IRC, WAIS, Finger, Ping etc. Usually, when you have access to the Internet through an ISP, you can use most or all of these tools if you should want to. Do not be alarmed, though – the useful ones are normally set up for you automatically, and most yachtsmen only ever use the three or four really important tools – **e-mail**, the **World Wide Web, FTP** and sometimes **newsgroups**.

As a yachtsman, which of these you use, and how often, will depend upon two factors: what kind of sailing you do, and what kind of Internet access you have.

E-mail

Electronic mail is a fantastically useful tool – allowing you to send and receive messages worldwide, at incredibly low cost; it can contain pictures, sounds, even videos. Even better, e-mail is an asynchronous (or store and forward) system – unlike the telephone, where both parties have to be present to conduct a conversation, once you have sent an e-mail, it waits on the recipient's 'mail server' (a kind of electronic post office) until they log in and collect it. If for any reason the e-mail doesn't arrive (maybe you misspelled the address?), the Internet will 'bounce' the e-mail back to you, so you know your message didn't get through.

Virtually all Internet users ashore have access to and use e-mail. On board, e-mail is often the only part of the Internet that yachtsmen currently use, because simple text messages do not require a fast connection. Assuming you have the relevant account set up and suitable equipment on board, it is quite possible to send and receive e-mail via a GSM mobile phone, INMARSAT C, M or Mini-M or MF/HF SSB radio.

With some modern satellite systems, you don't even need to have a PC on board to send and receive e-mail messages. However,

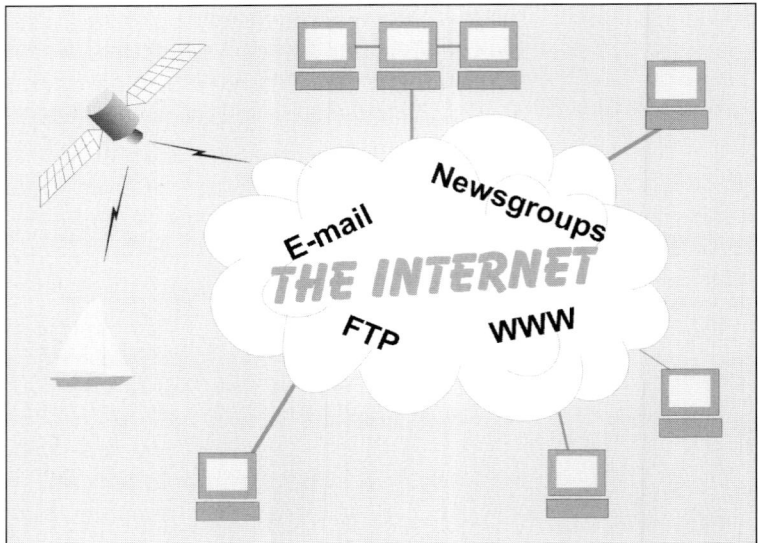

The Internet offers seamless connectivity between computers all over the world

even with these systems, using a PC with an available serial port makes life much simpler because you can use the PC's keyboard and access the system's functions much more easily.

For more information on communications including e-mail, see chapter 4.

The World Wide Web

Also known as the WWW or simply 'the web', the World Wide Web lets Internet users access or 'browse' web sites of prepared information. Virtually all marine equipment manufacturers now maintain web sites, containing product and price information as well as links to other web sites containing related information.

This can be an invaluable resource for marine users. Imagine the scenario when, for example, in an unfamiliar harbour with a failed water pump for your engine: connect to the Internet and access the engine manufacturer's web site, then browse their parts list and distributor list to ascertain the part you require and your nearest agent. You have a query? E-mail the technical department for further information. No local dealer? Order direct, pay by credit card and have the part shipped by courier.

WWW access requires a more powerful connection to the Internet than does e-mail, so access to the WWW when sailing offshore is currently restricted to superyachts and commercial vessels. Leisure yachtsmen *can* browse the WWW reasonably well from their PC, using a GSM cellphone, but if you do this, set your web browser to display just text, with all images and sound switched off, as this will significantly improve performance. Also, some well appointed marinas are offering a shore phone line, which eliminates any communications problems when you are tied up alongside.

This situation will improve over the next few years and it seems certain that very soon it will be possible (and affordable) for ordinary yachtsmen to enjoy the same kind of access speeds within cellphone range that they enjoy when ashore.

Beyond cellphone range, fast web browsing is unlikely to be within the pocket of the average yachtsman for some time to come.

FTP

File transfer protocol, or FTP, is a means of downloading information from the Internet to your PC. This may often be data, such as weather information, or programs, such as a demo version of an application or the latest software release. Access to FTP sites is generally made through your web browser, but if you use a separate FTP program you'll find that files generally download faster, as there is not all of the graphical interface of the web to be downloaded first. FTP also has the facilities allowing you to upload files, rename them, delete them and so on, subject to having the necessary access rights.

You will also find that there are still a few places on the Internet offering a service called remote FTP. This goes back to the early days of the Internet, when a fast modem was 2400 bps, and just about everything was text based. You send a specially formatted e-mail to a remote FTP server with details of the FTP site you want to access, and the files you want to retrieve from it. The server then automatically retrieves the file and sends it to you as an e-mail. This is still the only way to retrieve files if you have a store and forward system, such as INMARSAT C, and it is also generally more efficient than using the web or standard FTP.

Newsgroups

Most Internet users with ordinary dial-up access through an ISP automatically have access to newsgroups – even if they don't know it! Newsgroups are really giant noticeboards to which you can send messages which can then be read by anyone else who visits the newsgroup. In this way, 'threads' or topics of discussion are built up that you may simply read for interest or make your contribution to, if you have something constructive to offer the discussion.

There are an enormous number of newsgroups available to all Internet users – you can be more or less certain there will be groups that address your interests, marine or otherwise. Once you have found one that looks of interest, you 'subscribe' to it – this means that when you dial up, your news software automatically checks the newsgroup for messages that you have not seen yet, and downloads them onto your PC.

As you may imagine, some newsgroups are very active and some are less so; also the quality of discussion (as in real life) can vary enormously. Some newsgroups are unashamedly partisan to one cause or another and others may have overwhelmingly regional, particularly US, bias. However, many newsgroups are 'moderated' by a responsible individual to ensure discussions do not get out of hand or wander from the main thread.

Some very active newsgroups can generate a lot of traffic and for this reason, if you are using newsgroups on board, it is recommended that you subscribe to only those that are of very great interest – newsgroup browsing can be very addictive!

Internet connections from ashore

If you have a PC on board, but do not have a suitable communications system to access the Internet whilst at sea, you can still use your on board PC to prepare e-mail or fax messages for sending on once you reach your destination.

Usually, access to the Internet is achieved through a local-rate call to your ISP's Point of Presence (POP). Although it is possible to reach your normal POP through the international telephone exchanges, this could work out very costly – and you may need an extremely large number of coins if you are unable to use a credit card or calling card to make the call from a payphone. It makes sense therefore if you are planning to travel widely that you select an ISP which is able to offer local-rate call POPs in most, if not all, your intended destination countries.

Global ISPs and remote e-mail services

One way of getting round this problem is to use a remote e-mail service that you can use via the WWW. Then, all you have to do is to find somewhere you can get access to the WWW (probably using someone else's local-call rate access to their ISP) and to log in to your e-mail account. There are several of these services available, Microsoft's *Hotmail* (http://www.hotmail.com) was one of the earliest and is certainly the most popular with blue-water yachtsmen. At time of writing, *Hotmail* remains free of charge, though of course you will probably need to pay someone to get access to the WWW in order to access your account.

Another alternative is to use an ISP that has an international presence. A number of ISPs in different countries have banded together to be able to offer global roaming, which means that in most countries you do not have to make an international call (though there may be a slight surcharge levied to cover the extra costs involved in providing the service). Alternatively some of the bigger providers such as AOL and CompuServe have local points of presence in most countries, but often their highly graphical user interfaces mean that the link can be unreliable on a slow speed connection.

Hotel telephones

A laptop PC will let you take your data to the phone if you have a built-in modem (which very many do have). This is achieved by simply plugging the modem into a hotel room telephone socket, connecting to the international telephone network, and thence to the Internet.

Bear in mind, though, that there are many different socket types in use worldwide, and that if venturing far it would be wise to invest in one of the adapter sets which are seen at airports and telephone shops. Hotels, of course, have probably the most expensive phones it is possible to use, but in some areas hotels have better maintained lines than may be available otherwise.

Cybercafés

These are becoming very popular in far-flung parts of the world. The basic concept is that you pay a fee per hour or half-hour to access the WWW whilst enjoying a cup of coffee. Typically, a yachtsman would use his on board PC to prepare e-mail messages and would then save them on to a floppy disk that he takes to the local Internet café. Once there, he connects via the WWW to a remote e-mail system, such as *Hotmail* or *Bigfoot,* so he can send his messages. Whilst on-line, he can also receive any messages that have arrived since he last connected and save them onto disk to be read at leisure on the on board PC.

One might assume that this facility was confined to more developed parts of the world, but such is the penetration of the Internet that they can be found in cafés and bars, chandleries and harbour offices in the most unlikely and remote places.

Acoustic couplers

There are surprisingly few locations in the world where it is not possible to find a telephone – this is usually the first element of a modern infrastructure that reaches a place, often before mains electricity and sewage. Certainly in more developed parts of the world, it is unusual to be in a dock or harbour without a public telephone being within easy walking distance.

Once the *only* way to connect a computer modem to a phone line, acoustic couplers are nowadays far less common than they used to be, but having one on board could allow you to send e-mails from the most basic public payphone rather than using an expensive hotel phone.

A modem takes digital computer information and turns it into sounds that may be sent down a telephone wire. An acoustic coupler consists of two 'cups' that fit over the telephone mouthpiece and earpiece – it simply transfers the sounds between the telephone and the modem itself. Although inelegant and a little awkward to use, acoustic couplers can often be used where no other method would work.

9 • Choosing a PC System

Currently, it is unusual for marine software products to be sold with a PC included, or indeed for a PC to be sold 'bundled' with marine software. Some specialists do offer this service, which gives you the benefit of a complete, ready to go PC, and this is particularly useful if you want a system of any complexity or if you are new to computers.

Alternatively, if you shop around and buy the components separately you may get a better price (especially if you want a laptop-based solution), though you have the responsibility of making sure that all components of the system meet your needs and are compatible with each other.

In many cases, dealing with an experienced marine computing company that offers a total service will pay dividends in the long run and may cost you less than 'going direct'. This route often gives you better choice, more independent advice and good after-sales service.

First choice: hardware or software?

Deciding on which hardware and software to purchase may appear to be a confusing business, but essentially the process may be approached in one of two ways, and this depends upon whether you already own a PC or not:

If you already have a PC – Find out its specifications and then look for software that will run on it. If you do not already know them, you should be able to find out the PC's specifications from the manual you got when you bought it. Once you have done this, contact a dealer and ask for brochures or catalogues of the types of application you are interested in, and select from packages whose hardware requirements match those of the PC.

If you have not yet bought a PC – If you know which software you want to use, find out the software requirements as described above and then use this as a check-list against the PC specifications when deciding which PC to purchase. Bear in mind that you should always buy a PC that is a little more powerful than you need right now, or that can be upgraded in the future, in case new software comes along that has greater system requirements.

Either way, the key to this process is knowing the specifications of the PC, and the system requirements of the software that you want to run. The most important thing is that the PC must be powerful enough to run the software. If the software has requirements that exceed the specifications of the PC, it will not run correctly, if at all, so this is a very important stage in making a decision.

> **Tip** – Sometimes people who do not yet have a PC or software are tempted to buy a PC before choosing the software. This is really the wrong way round because you may end up having purchased a PC which is not powerful enough to do what you want it to, or you may have spent more than you had to on a PC that is far more powerful than you need.

You may have got the impression that you will need the latest and most powerful PC on board. This could not be further from the truth – typically, marine software is not as resource-hungry as other types (for example the latest games, multimedia or large office applications). So while software will always run faster on more powerful PCs, many yachtsmen experience perfectly acceptable performance when using an older, or even second-hand, PC on board.

Computer architecture

Before looking at the individual elements of a computer system, let us first look at the overall architecture of the system.

The 'bus' – linking it all together

Central to the PC is the bus, a kind of nervous system that lets all of the different components of the system talk to each other. In practice, there are a number of different buses in most computers, each with different functions and usually etched onto the 'motherboard'.

The way the different buses and boards are connected together in a PC varies very much according to the PC type – office PC, marine or industrial PC, and laptop.

The 'ISA' bus is the original PC bus, and is still used for some sound cards, serial cards and other cards that do not require high performance. Although Microsoft and Intel are trying to phase it out, it will probably survive for quite a while longer as there is a limit to the number of 'PCI' (see below) slots that can be installed in a machine.

After a few false starts by IBM and others, the PCI bus has emerged as the standard high performance bus for the PC. It is significantly

A typical PC motherboard, which carries the 'bus', linking together the system components

faster than the ISA bus partly because the data physically moves around much faster, and also because it was designed to allow cards to move data around more efficiently. Most new cards that are introduced these days are based on the PCI bus.

Whilst the ISA and PCI buses can take almost any type of expansion card, the AGP bus was devised exclusively for high performance graphics cards, allowing them to talk directly to the CPU. This allows the same graphics processor to run some 30% faster in the AGP version than in the PCI bus version. Whilst supported by Windows 98, the AGP bus is not currently supported by Windows NT4.

Disk drives are generally interfaced by the IDE bus, whereby each IDE interface can have one or two disks attached, and many PCs have two IDE interfaces. The Extended IDE (EIDE) interface, fitted as standard nowadays, has the ability to take ATAPI devices such as CD-ROM drives, and has the performance to match all but the fastest of 'SCSI' drives.

The SCSI interface has been widely used for high performance disk drives and CD-ROM drives, and is still extensively used for back-up tape drives and scanners. Its use is declining, due to the increased performance of the EIDE interface, and also the increase in 'USB' (see below), but when running Windows NT the use of SCSI hard disks enables the operating system to make the disk drive system both faster and more secure. It is also used for applications such as video recording, where the highest possible data transfer rate to the disks is required. SCSI is generally implemented through an add-in PCI bus card, and can take a number of devices connected on the same port, which can generally be used simultaneously.

The Universal Serial Bus (USB) has been fitted to laptop and desktop machines for quite a while now, but it is only recently that devices have appeared that can use it. USB allows a large number of devices to be connected together, with power as well as data being provided. For a desktop machine this means that you don't need a separate power socket for each device, but for a laptop it means even more drain on the laptop's limited battery capacity. Also, although there are teething problems, and the bus sometimes does not cope well with many devices working simultaneously, USB is almost certain to become a very common and important bus. USB devices at present are typically printers, scanners, digital cameras and modems.

Components of a PC system

The processor   At the core of the PC system is the CPU (central processing unit) or processor, which controls the system and performs all of the calculations necessary for programs to run. In the PC market the main manufacturer has been Intel, who have produced PC processors from the very earliest days of the PC. The early series of Intel processors such as 8086, 80286 (286), 80386 (386) and 80486 (486) are of historical interest, and the Pentium range is now offered. The first series of Pentiums have been phased out and the second range (Pentium MMX) is rapidly following. Many new machines have a Pentium II processor, and at the time of writing the Pentium III is current. Processors run at different speeds (measured in MHz), currently ranging from 233 to 750MHz – the higher the speed, the faster the PC runs. There is also a range of Celeron processors offering slightly reduced performance at lower cost.

Intel does not have a monopoly on processors though; AMD is becoming increasingly popular, particularly for entry level and mid range systems with their K2 and K3 ranges. Another manufacturer is Cyrix, but their processors currently lack a floating point unit (the part that does complex maths), which is needed by some marine applications, so this processor should be selected with caution. Note that different manufacturers measure the speed of their processors

The 'heart' of the PC, the CPU or processor

differently, so a 300MHz AMD processor does not run at the same speed as a 300MHz Pentium processor, for example. Also, as you will see later in this chapter, processor speed is not the only factor in the overall performance of your PC.

It is worth bearing in mind that the speed of computer processors doubles about every 18 months, which is why computers become obsolete fairly quickly. Very few laptops can have the processor upgraded, but many marine PCs use 'passive backplane' technology, which means that the processor is upgradeable. For some upgrades this simply involves replacing the processor, or if upgrading to a new series of processor, the card that the processor is fitted on may need replacing as well.

Memory (RAM)

When a program is running, as much of the program and its data as possible is copied from the PC's hard disk into Random Access Memory (RAM). This is because it is over a hundred times quicker to read data into the processor from RAM than it is from a hard disk, and a thousand times quicker than from a CD-ROM drive. however, if the program is large, or you are running several programs at once, your PC may not have enough RAM. In this case, the PC will start 'paging' to free up more memory. This consists of discarding from RAM bits of the program or data that are not currently in use, to make room for those bits that are needed next. Then, when the discarded bits are required again, they are read back in from the hard disk into RAM. Although this is a wasteful process, it allows large programs to run in small amounts of RAM.

RAM chips, packaged as SIMMs or DIMMs, store data while the PC is switched on

The obvious thing to do is to fit as much RAM as possible into your PC – 16 megabytes (Mb) is the absolute minimum that should be fitted, but 64 or 128Mb is becoming the norm. This will keep your entire program in memory, and adding more memory can be a far more cost effective way of increasing your PC's performance than fitting a faster processor. The memory generally comes on small cards holding a number of chips on them, which slot in to sockets in the PC. There are a number of different formats and specifications for memory, so it is worth checking with your computer supplier when upgrading.

Storage – disks and discs

A computer's RAM memory has two major disadvantages – when the computer is switched off the memory is cleared; and it is difficult to distribute programs or data on memory. For these reasons, a number of disk formats are used for longer term storage.

Hard disk

The hard disk (or drive) is used for permanent storage of programs and data on the PC as well as 'paging' as described. Disk capacity typically extends from 3Gb to 15Gb, and machines other than laptops can generally have up to 4 hard disks installed in them, or many more SCSI disks.

When you first get a new machine, it will probably have much more disk space than its predecessor, and you'll think you will never fill it up. However, as operating systems and programs get larger, you will almost inevitably find that sooner or later it will be almost full, and this will cause problems with larger programs and when printing. It is generally much easier to add another disk to a machine than to replace an existing disk with a larger one since most desktop and marine PCs can support several hard disks at once.

Floppy disk

A hard disk is fine in one machine, but they cannot easily be transferred between machines. The floppy disk has long been the standard means of distributing and transferring files and data, though for program distribution it is losing out to the CD-ROM (see below). The standard disk size is the Double Sided High Density (DSHD) 3.5" disk, with a 1.44Mb capacity.

Larger/optical discs

Reflecting the fact that these days 1.44Mb is very small, a variety of higher capacity disc formats have emerged, one of the more notable being Iomega's Zip drive (holding around 100Mb). The large format 'floppy disk' is an appealing concept, but because there are many different incompatible formats, and only a minority of PCs have the necessary hardware fitted as standard, these are not very useful for transferring data between computers.

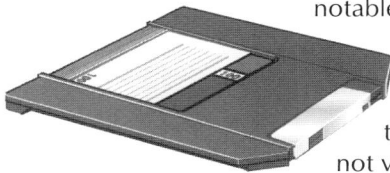

CD-ROM and DVD discs

As programs and data sizes have got larger, the floppy disk has largely been replaced by the CD-ROM – for the publisher it is also a more reliable and lower cost medium than a floppy disk. Some programs, in particular games, will often run directly from the CD-ROM, but most office and marine programs are installed from the CD-ROM to the hard disk. This is just as well, as CD-ROM drives are all significantly slower than hard disks, and also are not very reliable when the boat is bouncing around at sea.

A CD-ROM has a maximum storage capacity of 640Mb, but can come in a number of different types or 'formats'. The most common is the CD-ROM, which are pressed from a glass master in large quantities. With a suitable drive, users can also create their own CDs, which can then be read by all but the oldest of CD-ROM drives. The most common format is CD-R (also known as 'gold' CDs due to their original colour, though this is often silver or metallic blue or green now). With this the CD can only be written to once, which is ideal for long term archival storage of programs or data. The other is CD-RW, which is a rewriteable format, which can also be used for back-up purposes. With CD-RW discs, when a file is deleted using Microsoft Windows it is not actually deleted from the CD-RW until it is wiped clean, by 'reformatting' or 'initialising', so with time the disc can fill up with deleted files.

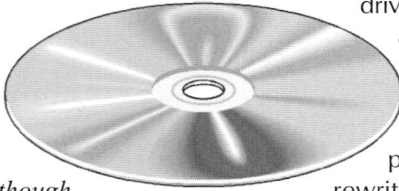

Although identical, DVDs can store several times more data than a CD-ROM

The latest variation on this theme is the Digital Versatile Disc (DVD), which is the same physical size as the CD-ROM/CD-R, but the present capacity is about 5 times greater, and this is set to double when double sided drives appear. At present these are mainly used for distributing films, but this format is sure to replace the CD-ROM in time. DVD drives read CDs and DVDs. As well as the standard DVD disc, it is now possible to get DVD-RAM drives, which allow you to create your own discs in the same way as CD-R discs.

The display

Almost all displays used on leisure boats are flat panel displays – they will either be built into a laptop PC or supplied as separate displays – for example, for bulkhead mounting. Flat panels have recently dropped in price quite markedly, and have also become available in larger sizes. Compared with traditional cathode ray tube (CRT) displays, flat panel displays offer greater reliability, more compact size and lower power consumption which makes them ideal for the job.

Traditional cathode ray tube (CRT) display (left) and a TFT (thin film transistor) display panel (right)

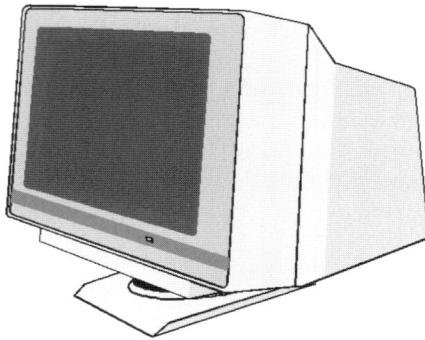

Choosing a display

When choosing a flat panel display, consider the following factors:

◆ **The physical size**, measured diagonally from corner to corner. Flat panel display sizes specify the actual viewable dimension, but CRT monitors measure that larger dimension to the corners of the glass tube. Most laptops offer a 12.1" display (corresponding to a 14" CRT display) – this is the smallest practical size. At the other end, TFT displays up to 18", or even up to 60" (using 'plasma' technology), are available.

◆ **The resolution**, measured in pixels (dots) across and down the display. This is generally tied in with the screen size, so 12.1" displays are generally 800x600 resolution (also known as SVGA), with smaller displays at 640x480 resolution (VGA), and 14" and larger displays at 1024x768 or higher (XGA). Note that flat screens display resolutions lower than their maximum in one of two ways: some display a smaller image on the screen, with a black surround, others expand the smaller image to the full display size (sometimes resulting in a slight loss of sharpness in the image).

◆ **The number of colours**. Early flat screens could only display 256 colours simultaneously, which was quite limiting on graphics programs. Now, most will show thousands, if not millions, of colours, depending upon the amount of graphics memory fitted to the PC's display adapter (often 2, 4 or 8Mb).

◆ **The technology**. Most common is the TFT display, which is what we would recommend for normal use. Less expensive is the STN (or dual scan) display; this responds more slowly to signals from the computer, so the mouse may be hard to see when moving. STN displays also have a smaller range of viewing angles than do TFT displays and are not recommended for use on board. Finally, there is the transflective or reflective display, which is ideal for use on deck as it excels in bright light conditions, using a mirror behind the display to illuminate it rather than a backlight.

◆ **The brightness**. For marine use, a display must be bright enough to be seen in bright light and capable of being dimmed right down in darkness to maintain the user's night vision. The brightness of a display is measured in candela/m^2 (also known as NITS in the USA). Most office grade and laptop displays are rated at around 150–200 candela/m^2. Marine grade displays are available at two ratings: about 300 candela/m^2 for use in areas sheltered from direct sunlight, and 1500 candela/m^2 or more to ensure that the display can be read in direct sunlight.

Quite often on a bigger boat you may want a number of repeater displays. This can easily be arranged by using a video splitter. Alternatively, multiple screens can be used with more flexibility if you use Windows 98's ability to support multiple PCI bus graphics cards, or one of the multi-port graphics cards that are available. Note that in general all flat screens in the system will need to be of the same resolution.

In office machines, there is a trend to using an AGP bus graphics card, as this offers a performance edge over PCI bus cards. However, it must be noted that these cards are not currently supported by Windows NT4, which requires a PCI or ISA bus card.

Keyboard

Many marine programs are designed so the primary input mechanism is the mouse, rather than the keyboard. However, most programs need keyboard input at some stage, so it is essential to have a keyboard available, even if most of the time it is tucked away.

Even if you are using a laptop, which of course includes a built-in keyboard, it is still often sensible to add an external keyboard. Basic keyboards are so cheap (typically under £10.00) that they can be regarded as sacrificial and are a very good way of keeping the laptop dry. As well as normal office-type keyboards, very compact, water resistant and fully waterproof keyboards can be purchased from marine computing specialists.

Replacement keyboards are so cheap, they can be regarded as sacrificial

PS/2 connectors are used for keyboards and mice

There are two types of connector commonly used for keyboards, the older AT type uses a 5-pin DIN connector (shown in the picture on the facing page), while more modern keyboards use the smaller and more reliable PS/2 connector. Laptop PCs are almost universally fitted with a PS/2 connector, whilst office-type PCs may have a mixture. Adapters are freely available from computer stores to convert between the two kinds of connector.

Many laptops include only one PS/2 connector, which can be used for an external keyboard or a mouse. Usually it is possible to purchase a 'Y' connector, which allows both a keyboard and a mouse to share the same connector on the laptop (check your PC manual to confirm this will work with your computer).

A wireless keyboard is often very useful, as it can be stowed away without having to unplug anything. Radio-based wireless keyboards are preferred to infra-red ones, as the radio signals can pass through non-metallic objects, whereas infra-red beams are easily blocked by objects, or can be unreliable in very bright light.

Pointing devices

Some method of pointing at objects on the PC screen is essential with most marine programs. On board, this is usually accomplished using a mouse or a trackball, though other methods, such as touch-screens and light pens, may be used.

Trackballs are usually preferred to mice, because they can be secured so as not to slide around the navigation area. Some (slightly more expensive) trackballs work by monitoring an optical pattern on the ball itself, rather than by the ball turning small wheels within the mouse. Optical trackballs are better than the traditional type because they work more reliably with damp fingers.

Though more expensive than mice, track balls are to be preferred on board because they stay in one place

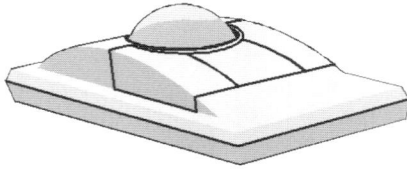

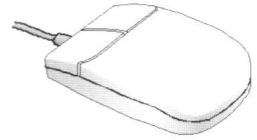

On some old PCs and laptops, the mouse was connected using a 9-pin serial port, rather than a dedicated PS/2 connector. Although this is very unusual nowadays, watch out for it because if the mouse is occupying your laptop's only serial port, you will not be able to use the PC for chart plotting or communications.

As with keyboards, wireless ones can be very useful and it is possible to buy combined keyboard/mouse wireless packages.

Although the idea of using a touch-screen is appealing, they often don't work well on board, for a number of reasons. Firstly, since your fingertip is often larger than the item you are trying to select on the screen, they can be inaccurate to use on a moving vessel. Secondly, depending upon the technology used, touch-screens can be ineffective with wet or damp fingers. Finally, and most importantly, many marine programs take advantage of the fact that mice typically have two buttons, using 'left-clicks' and 'right-clicks' to perform different tasks. A touch-screen is generally only able to provide a single click (usually interpreted by the software as a left-click). Some touch-screen manufacturers get around this by providing an on-screen button which when pressed means 'the next click is a right-click', but unless the marine software has been specifically designed around touch-screen limitations, it is likely to be pretty inconvenient to use on a regular basis.

Serial ports

The serial port on the PC is usually a 9-pin 'D' shaped connector (below left), although a few older PCs may be fitted with a 25-pin male 'D' connector (below right). Serial ports are often referred to as COM (for 'communication') ports and will be numbered, ie COM1, COM3, COM8 etc. You may also hear serial ports referred to as RS-232 ports, after the technical standard they are based on.

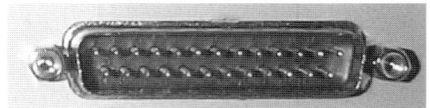

Serial ports are used extensively in marine computing for connecting the PC to navigation instruments, radio receivers, mobile phones etc. Most laptops are fitted with one serial port, most desktops with two, which is fine for simple set-ups, but finding enough ports on the PC may be a problem in more complex systems.

Microsoft Windows can support a large number of serial ports, and it is usually possible to fit additional serial ports (using a PC Card on a laptop PC or an ISA or PCI card on a desktop PC); however, the situation sadly is not that simple.

The first problem is that many programs are written to interface to COM1 or COM2 only. Secondly, each port needs its own dedicated 'interrupt' (IRQ), and on most PC-type computers IRQs are in very limited supply. Finally, there may not be the physical space to install an 'expansion' card in the PC.

To get around these important limitations, manufacturers are starting to use other methods of making the PC communicate with external equipment. Amongst these are sound cards, NMEA multiplexers, USB (Universal Serial Bus) as well as new networking technologies borrowed from the automotive industry (CAN).

Printer ports

Most PCs are fitted with one or two printer ports (usually one). Printer ports are also often called parallel ports because of the way data is transmitted using them. The connector on the PC is a 25-pin female 'D' shaped connector. The older 'Centronics' style connector used to be fitted to PCs as the printer port, but nowadays is only to be found on the printer itself.

25-pin printer port on the PC – note the holes, rather than pins

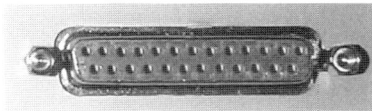

The printer port is much more flexible than its name suggests. As well as using it to connect the PC to a printer, a range of devices such as tape drives and scanners can also be plugged in to the printer port. Most of these devices have a 'pass-through' capability, so a number of other devices could in theory be connected onto the same port; however, the use of a printer port for these devices normally means that speed is not as great as if they were connected to a SCSI, PCI or IDE card.

Many electronic chart manufacturers protect their charts against illegal copying through the use of a hardware 'security key' or

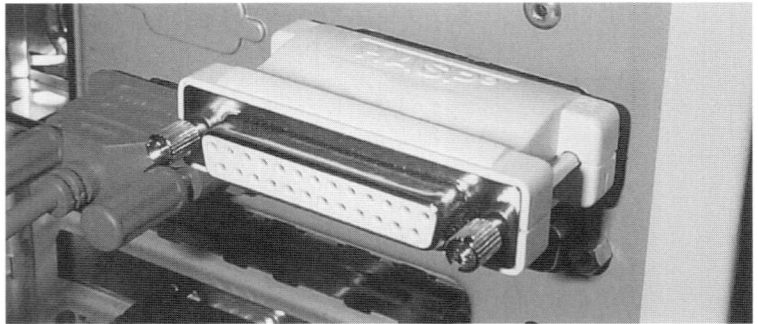

Dongle inserted in PC's printer port. Note connector on rear of dongle to plug printer into it

'dongle'. Most dongles take advantage of this pass-through capability and are connected to the PC using the printer port, thus allowing it to be used for a connection to a printer as well.

Unfortunately, some of the more modern printer drivers can cause problems when a dongle or another device wants to access the port, and the printer driver may need to be temporarily disabled. This is because some printer manufacturers ignore the Windows programming guidelines, and assume they are the only device using the port. This does not let other programs find their dongle or their hardware on the port, as the printer driver never lets their software look at the printer port.

PC Cards (PCMCIA)

All laptops these days have two PC Card (formerly called PCMCIA) sockets. PC Card readers are also available for desktop-type PCs, although they are not very common. These credit card-sized cards

PC Card half inserted in its slot. Most laptops can take two thinner cards or one fatter one

slot into the sockets on the PC and give access to a wide range of extra hardware – for example, modems for a land line or mobile phone, or networking capabilities. Other add-ons include extra serial ports, sound and video capture cards etc. On board, their greatest uses are in adding extra serial ports, and for a fax/data card for a mobile phone.

Operating systems

The operating system is the interface between the program you want to run, and the computer's hardware. It lets you and your programs read and write to files, display things on the screen, print things out, and also often provides a common appearance and style of interaction between you and the PC.

If you buy a PC today it will generally be supplied with Microsoft's Windows 98 installed. The earlier Windows 95 is virtually identical, differing mainly in the screen appearance, and in not having as much Internet functionality built in. In fact, many software and PC manufacturers now refer to the two products as being Windows 9x, where the 'x' stands for 5 or 8.

The previous family of Windows 3.0, 3.1 and Windows for Workgroups were developed for the earlier generation of 286, 386 and 486 processors, but most programs written for them will also run under Windows 95 and 98. Going back to the days before Windows there was MS-DOS (and even current versions of Windows run on top of a minimal subset of MS-DOS). A large proportion of MS-DOS programs will run under Windows, but it is worth noting that some of these, in particular graphics intensive games programs, can mess up your computer's configuration.

An alternative to Windows 98 is Windows NT (shortly to be replaced by Windows 2000). This operating system is geared more towards the business environment. Because of this, not as many multimedia and entertainment devices work under NT as under 95/98 (particularly, features such as AGP graphics cards, power saving features in laptops, and PC Card drivers, are not well supported, though the latest Service Pack 5 has improved some of these areas). NT, though, is generally a more robust system than 95/98, and its security features mean that for larger vessel installations, unauthorised crew members can be prevented from messing about with the computer configuration, installing unauthorised programs, and accessing or deleting files they should not.

The stated intention of Microsoft is to merge these two threads of Windows 98 and Windows NT into a common operating system, Windows 2000. When launched, this will have major internal differences between it and its two predecessors, so we can expect this to be followed up by Windows 2000 specific versions of programs.

Although under the same Windows brand name, it should be noted that Windows CE is a totally separate operating system from the rest of the Windows family. Applications written to operate under Windows CE will not run under other versions of Windows, and vice versa.

Another family of operating systems that runs on PCs is based on UNIX, which offered many of the facilities of Windows long before Windows came into existence. There are many variations of UNIX – Solaris, Xenix, AIX and Linux to name a few. Whilst the public domain Linux is increasing in popularity, it requires considerably more expertise to install and run than Windows, and there is little available software for the marine market that runs under it. Other operating systems include IBM's OS/2, and the Macintosh's System 7.

OK, so what should I buy?

With the rapid rate of hardware development, you have to accept that whatever you buy will be significantly cheaper, or maybe even redundant, within months of buying it. Also, if you want to buy leading edge technology you will pay a price premium – it is often worth staying one step back from the latest developments to enjoy large cost savings.

For an entry level system we would recommend the following minimum specification: Pentium 266MHz CPU, 32Mb RAM, 4Gb hard disk, CD-ROM drive, Windows 98. The display should be a minimum of a 12.1" 800x600 display.

This should meet basic requirements for the next couple of years. If you want a machine with a longer life expectancy it's worth considering a marine PC, since with these, individual components can be upgraded as required.

When you have decided how powerful you want your PC to be, you still have to face the choice of what general type – laptop, office or marine PC – you want to have on board. This will often be obvious due to personal preference, your budget and the physical space available on your boat. You may, however, find the following of use in deciding the shape of 'the package' that you purchase.

Laptop

Most first-time users of PCs on board start with a laptop computer, and this statistic speaks for itself. A laptop PC has all of its parts integrated onto a single board, which results in a portable and compact system.

There are a some drawbacks with laptops: first, upgrading system components is seldom possible, and for repairs you are totally dependent on the length of time the manufacturer stocks spares. Secondly, it can be hard to expand a laptop because all you have is PC Card and USB slots, and peripherals of these types are usually less versatile and more expensive than ISA or PCI slots. Finally, should the machine need repairing this is likely to be relatively expensive, and the machine will need sending back to the dealer for repairs.

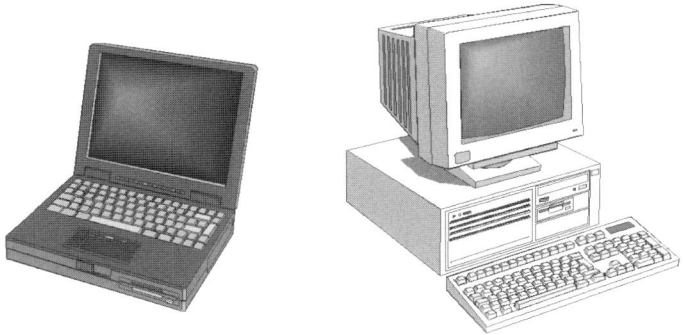

Both laptop and marine PCs may have a place on board your vessel

The big advantages of a laptop are its small size and portability. When not sailing, you can easily whisk the machine off the boat and back to the home or office, and if you do not use the machine on board all of the time it can easily be stowed away in a locker.

Office PC

An office-type desktop or mini-tower PC has the CPU and the common peripherals all installed on a common board, the 'motherboard' or 'mainboard' (this typically encompasses the keyboard and mouse ports, serial and printer ports, USB port and IDE ports, together with expansion slots for AGP, PCI and IDE boards). Integrating these common elements makes the system cheap to produce, but a drawback is that if the motherboard needs repairs or maintenance, the whole PC will need to be dismantled; in fact, as prices fall, it is often cheaper and more convenient to replace the PC than to attempt to repair a motherboard.

PCs designed for home or office use are intended to be mounted in a static, upright position. Although the low price of such a computer makes it tempting to use on a boat, its design makes it vulnerable to damage from vibration and constant motion.

Marine PC

The marine PC is generally based on an industrial PC architecture. The key point here is that instead of using a motherboard, a 'passive backplane' is used. This consists of a simple baseboard with ISA and PCI bus expansion slots, with a combined PCI/ISA slot to allow the processor to be mounted on a card that is simply plugged in like any other expansion card. This makes it very easy to maintain, repair and upgrade the system.

The processor board generally has a minimum of the processor, memory, IDE ports, serial and parallel ports mounted on it. Depending on the system requirements, they can also be supplied with networking, SCSI bus and graphics card functionality all built in. This increased integration results in a saving in the number of boards required, which then results in a more compact machine.

Marine PCs generally have all of the components better secured than desktop machines, with shock mounted drives, and 12V or 24VDC power supplies. They may well be more compact than a typical desktop or mini-tower-type domestic PC and will usually be fitted with strong mounting lugs, so the unit may be securely fixed to the vessel (via shock-absorbing mountings).

Front panel of a typically robust marine PC

Using a PC on board is as straightforward as using one ashore; however, there are some special environmental factors that need to be considered when planning the installation. Also, power supply and interfacing requirements should be planned.

Planning the installation

There are a number of options when it comes to installing your PC, largely based on the hardware option you have chosen – whether a desktop, laptop or a marine PC.

Unfortunately, few boats are designed to take a laptop at the chart table, which is generally the most obvious place to site it. Assuming you do not have the space to mount it permanently, the best solution is to have a cradle built, or a drawer or 'letter box' slot that it can be kept in, preferably with all of the cables connected. Failing this, you will have the chore of disconnecting the cabling each time you want to stow the laptop away.

The best way to secure the laptop is often to use Velcro strips underneath it, with the hooks on the laptop and the soft tape on the chart table. However, when doing this you need to ensure that you are not blocking any ventilation slots or covering up any of the catches found on many laptops.

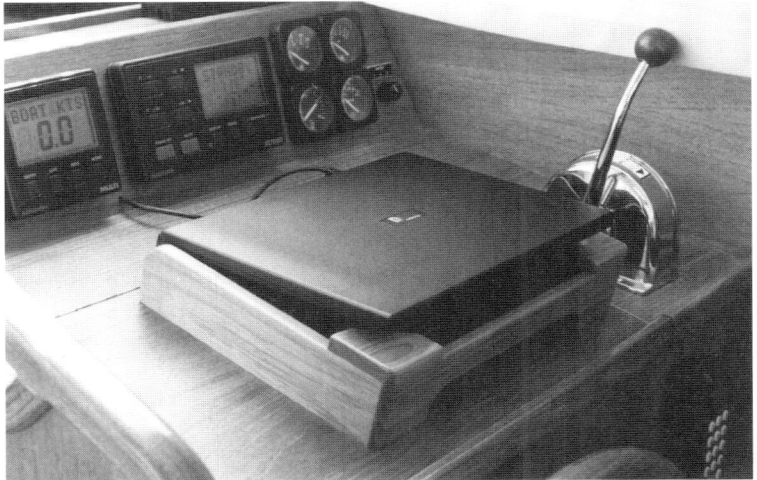

A particularly elegant 'cradle' designed to hold the laptop securely in place

If you have opted to have a separate display, keyboard and mouse connected to the laptop, installation is in many ways much easier. The laptop can be located out of the way in a locker or in the chart table, again secured with Velcro or a strap over the top; if you have a power switch mounted remotely then you will seldom need to access the laptop itself. With the low cost of TFT flat panel displays nowadays, this is a very popular solution – and still allows you to take your PC home when you leave the boat. The only points to watch are that the locker must not be damp, and must have reasonable ventilation.

Marine PCs are designed to be easy to install; most are supplied with mounting rails to secure them in place. As with a laptop, a marine PC needs to be located in a compartment with ventilation holes, and not in a compartment that gets too hot – the recommended maximum internal operating temperature is about 55° C, and the PC will generally run about 10° warmer than the surrounding air. On a marine PC, cooling fans are normally filtered to minimise dust ingress, so the filters will need cleaning or replacing periodically.

Screens and keyboards

When deciding on where to locate a flat screen display, consideration needs to be given to its viewing characteristics. TFT displays can typically be read at angles of up to 60°–80° off centre each side, and 10°–20° up and down. If angles greater than this are required, then you may want to mount the display on an adjustable tilt and swivel mount. If the screen has a reflective surface, you will also need to minimise glare from reflected lights.

The other major consideration with a display is its brightness. Below decks, or protected from bright light, a display with a brightness of 150–300 candela/m^2 (or NITS) will be adequate, but in bright light or direct sunlight a brightness of 1000 candela/m^2 will be required to allow the screen to be read in direct light. Also, consideration needs to be given to the screen's ability to be dimmed down, for if it cannot be dimmed right down then it should not be mounted in the line of vision of the helmsman or other crew members on watch at night.

The screen needs to be connected to the video output of the PC with good-quality video cable – too poor a quality and there will be 'ghosting', shown by text looking as though it has a shadow to it. For cable runs over about 15 metres, a video booster will be needed. With higher-quality laptops, the screen can run at a differ-

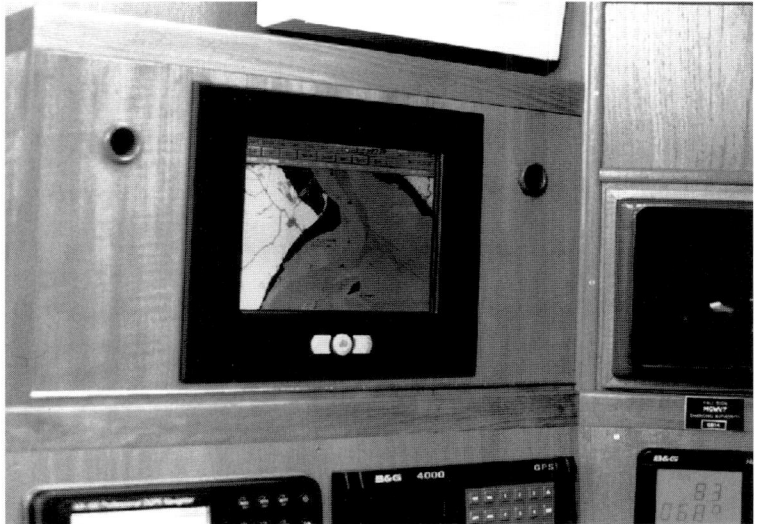

Here, in a well-designed navigation area, the marine PC is given pride of place

ent resolution from the laptop's screen, but with many the two must run at the same resolution, so you will need to match the screen to the laptop.

The keyboard and pointing device can either be console mounted, with a keyboard and trackball let into the surface of the chart table, or left free on the top. If console mounted, keyboards and mice should be mounted on a near horizontal surface – when operating them on vertical surfaces one's hand is cocked up at an impractica-ble and uncomfortable angle.

With separate keyboards and mice, the cables can be broken so as to have sockets at the rear of the chart table to plug the actual devices into. Instead of a mouse, consider a trackball secured to the chart table with the ubiquitous Velcro, as this will not roll around with the boat's movement. Alternatively, with a cordless keyboard and mouse the items can simply be placed in a drawer when not in use, but if the link is infra-red then there must be no obstructions when in use, or if it is a radio link then there must be no metal obstructions.

Environmental considerations

It is possible to purchase completely ruggedised and waterproofed equipment, built to tough military standards, but of course this is rarely within the budget of the typical yachtsman. However, by addressing the major environmental enemies of electronic equipment on board a seagoing vessel, and taking other commonsense precautions, it is perfectly reasonable to anticipate a long and reliable life from most modern PCs on board.

Shock and vibration

The insides of a computer, and its disk drive, are generally much more shock resistant than most people realise, and on most boats no special precautions need to be taken. On a well designed marine PC, designed with a configuration that anticipates high shock loadings, expansion and motherboards are mounted vertically; if it uses a Pentium II processor this will be mounted parallel to its processor board, as opposed to the normal right angle mounting on domestic PCs.

For high-speed vessels or those operating in very harsh conditions, the PC can be mounted on anti-shock mounts, which will also help to avoid vibration problems. Regardless of how the PC is mounted, the CD-ROM drive and floppy disk drive will not operate well in severe conditions, so it is wise to have all important programs and data (charts etc) loaded onto the PC before you encounter these conditions.

Vibration can be a more insidious problem, with the potential for components to slowly work loose with time. Whilst all internal boards in a PC have a retaining screw at one end, in a marine PC the whole board is locked down by a retaining strap and guide over the boards at the other end, locking everything in place. Also, installation details such as having cables to the PC secured down will help avoid their shaking loose. Most customers prefer to avoid non-standard screw-in or lock-in cable connectors being used, as these increase costs and mean that standard PC cables and components cannot be used.

Temperature

The maximum operating temperature of most PC components is typically about 55–60° C. You may think that your equipment will not reach this temperature, but because it is air cooled it requires the surrounding air to be 10° C cooler or more. Because of this, it is essential that the equipment is mounted in a vented locker, and that fans and air vents are not blocked. Whilst a good-quality marine PC can monitor its internal temperature, and in some cases also generate a high temperature alarm, with other equipment you are relying on good installation practice.

If the equipment is mounted where it is exposed to sunlight, then heating from solar radiation can also be significant. The heating effect will be at a maximum in the tropics, when the sun is high above the horizon, and the exposed surface is at right angles to the sun's rays. It is also more of a problem for components with a dark matt finish, fitted in a metal casing with high thermal conductivity.

LCD displays have their own particular problems in temperature extremes. At sub-zero temperatures the display may initially fail to operate, though they normally heat up quickly. At very high temperatures the display may black out, particularly when heated by the sun. This can be solved by gently cooling it with seawater, or by strategically placing a crew member to keep it in the shade.

It should also be noted that if LCDs are operated at high temperatures, this will also have a long term effect of shortening the life of the panel (it will rapidly become dim with age). High temperature problems are particularly likely to occur with high brightness displays that are not fitted with a cooling fan, since the backlight and electronics output a lot of heat into a small enclosed space, which will overheat on deck when exposed to warm weather and a bright sun.

Humidity

Humidity on its own can cause problems with condensation forming and shorting out components, connections or wires, but when coupled with a salt atmosphere, salt crystals in the air are deposited on the components and cause additional corrosion. Laptops are particularly prone to these problems, because having everything compressed into such a small place means that connectors are relatively small and more prone to corrosion problems. Also, they do not have the filtered fans of a marine PC, so it is easier for salt crystals in the atmosphere to enter the PC. However, with almost all computer equipment the motherboards are coated to protect against corrosion.

Apart from keeping the boat's atmosphere as dry as possible, a useful tip is to keep equipment running continuously when on board, keeping a constant working temperature inside the unit.

When the PC is switched off it cools down, encouraging salty, corrosive condensation to form. When switched back on, the increase in temperature makes this condensation more corrosive until it has evaporated off.

Power supply

Running a PC on board requires both a good-quality and reliable power source. In fact, the power source is at least as important as the PC, which will be useless unless it has sufficient electrical power to run.

There are various methods of supplying power to your PC while your vessel is under way, but some methods may not be as effective or electrically efficient as others.

Internal computer batteries

All laptop and notebook PCs have interchangeable, rechargeable batteries. Until recently, one could expect fairly short running times of around an hour or two. However, significant improvements in power storage technology have greatly extended operating times to around four or five hours in a typical laptop. This is even the case with today's large, high resolution, bright TFT screens that are notoriously power-hungry.

Four or five hours of operation is fine for an occasional day sail, especially if fully charged spare batteries are kept close to hand. Yachtsmen who rely on their PC for navigation, however, will require longer operating times and therefore will either need several spares or a method of charging the PC's internal batteries whilst away from shore power.

DC-DC converters

Various DC-DC converters are commercially available. These are generally made up of a cigarette lighter attachment and a plug to fit into the PC's DC power socket. They operate by converting the boat's 12VDC or 24VDC supply to the operating voltage of the PC. When laptop PCs first became common, suitable DC-DC converters were hard to find, but as the market for laptops has expanded, many branded as well as after-market units are available, aimed mainly at the executive with a company car.

Whilst ideal for in-car use, DC-DC converters suffer a number of drawbacks in the marine environment:

◆ Most DC-DC converters only provide DC power to the PC to operate it, they do not charge the batteries at the same time. This is significant since the PC's internal batteries can provide a valuable 'get you home' safety margin, should the boat's DC supply fail (assuming you also have spare batteries for your GPS set!).

◆ DC-DC converters by-pass the PC's own power supply unit (PSU) and provide DC power directly to the PC's motherboard. In the event of a high voltage spike from the yacht's electrical system or a fault occurring in the converter itself, the motherboard may get damaged. If a non-manufacturer-approved DC-DC converter has been used, this will almost certainly invalidate the PC's warranty.

◆ The method of connection to the yacht's electrical system is not very reliable – usually, a cigar lighter socket or similar is used and this may not have a fuse of a suitable rating fitted.

◆ DC-DC converters are not always available in 24VDC for commercial or larger boat use.

◆ Some DC-DC converters may cause interference to weatherfax and weathersat reception

DC to AC power inverters

Inverters convert 12 or 24VDC power from the boat's batteries to 230VAC mains electricity. This allows the PC to operate in exactly the same way as if it were plugged into the mains at home. If you are using a laptop PC, an inverter is certainly the preferred option because it provides valuable charging of the PC's own batteries. In any case, having an inverter on board allows the use of other AC devices such as printers, mobile phones, VHF radio chargers etc. It may even be cheaper to buy an inverter than several 'car chargers'.

> **Warning** – Inverters produce AC electrical power at 120–240V. **This is sufficient to kill** and is more hazardous than dealing with 12 or 24VDC electrical power on board. There are also many different inverter technologies available, so care must be taken to ensure that a suitable inverter is chosen. Unless you are familiar with marine electrics, this is an area where it is usually best to consult with an expert before purchasing an inverter.

Efficiency

On a boat with limited power generation capability, it is extremely important that losses of electrical energy are kept to an absolute minimum. This has traditionally been a reason for not using an inverter, since older models were notoriously inefficient. Happily, the situation is now much better, with most inverter manufacturers quoting efficiency percentages in the mid nineties. With a modern, correctly installed inverter, there is no reason why the yachtsman can't have a reasonable quantity of good-quality AC power available on board at all times.

What size inverter?
As a rough guide, the following sizes of inverter should be used for different PCs:

Inverter size	Type of PC	Other Uses
75–150W	Notebook	Bubblejet printer, mobile phone/VHF charger
250–500W	Desktop/Marine	As above + televisions and small power tools
1000–2000W	As above	Laser printer, plotter and most domestic appliances

If planning to use an inverter in excess of 150W it is essential to check the yacht's DC electrical system and battery capacity to ensure they are capable of coping with the electrical load that would result from using the inverter at full power. Such an inverter should be placed on its own DC electrical circuit and be protected with a suitably rated fuse and/or breaker.

Modified v pure sine-wave inverters
There are essentially two types of AC electrical output produced by inverters; these are known as modified (or stepped, quasi or trapezoidal) sine-wave and pure sine-wave.

AC electricity, when plotted on a graph, gives a smooth wave shape that looks rather like a radio wave. Modified sine-wave units attempt to provide a similar-looking waveform with a number of steps up and back down again. Laptop and desktop PCs will usually operate well from a modified sine-wave inverter. However, a pure sine-wave inverter is often required for many specialist, and even some 'standard', PC monitors.

Modified sine-wave inverters attempt to model a pure sine-wave in small steps

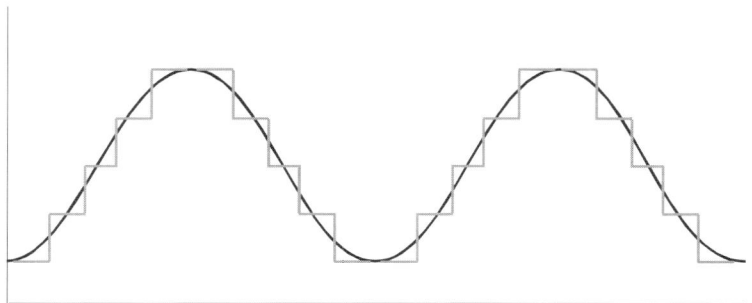

The table below compares modified and pure sine-wave inverters:

	Pure Sine	Modified Sine
Cost	*	*****
Operating efficiency	*****	****
Running notebooks	*****	****
Running desktops	*****	*
Running bubblejet printer	*****	****
Running laser printers	*****	*
Interference	*****	*,
Running other peripherals	*****	****

Key: 1 * = poor, 5 * = excellent

In fact, when choosing an inverter, it is not as simple as deciding between modified or pure sine-wave output, because there are also three types of power conversion technology used in inverters. The power conversion technology used has a great bearing on the efficiency, life and interference produced by the inverter – as well, of course, as on its cost.

It may help to understand the benefits and drawbacks of the main conversion technologies:

1 Ferroresonant
This type of inverter uses a large transformer and fairly basic circuitry to provide AC power. such inverters are generally very reliable but are not recommended for use on boats as their efficiency is poor.

2 Switch mode
This type of inverter is much smaller, lighter and efficient than other units. Most switch-mode inverters are of the modified sine-wave type. They are ideal for marine use; however, they are not as reliable as ferroresonant types and can produce interference if not installed correctly.

3 Hybrid
The latest inverter technology combines a hybrid transformer with a switch-mode design. These are much more reliable than switch-mode units yet still retain excellent reliability and produce low interference. They are often more expensive and generally produce a pure sine-wave.

A small inverter may be powerful enough for a laptop PC

In summary, inverters are the preferred method of providing power for laptop PCs. A modern laptop PC with fairly modest power requirements can be driven from a 75W inverter, not much larger than a packet of cigarettes, though some more powerful machines may require a 150W inverter.

If you have a desktop or marine PC on board, you will probably need a larger inverter, at least 250W. This is where there is the greatest choice in terms of output waveforms and power conversion technology available and, given a suitable DC electrical system to back it up, a larger inverter can be used to power many other devices on board as well as a PC.

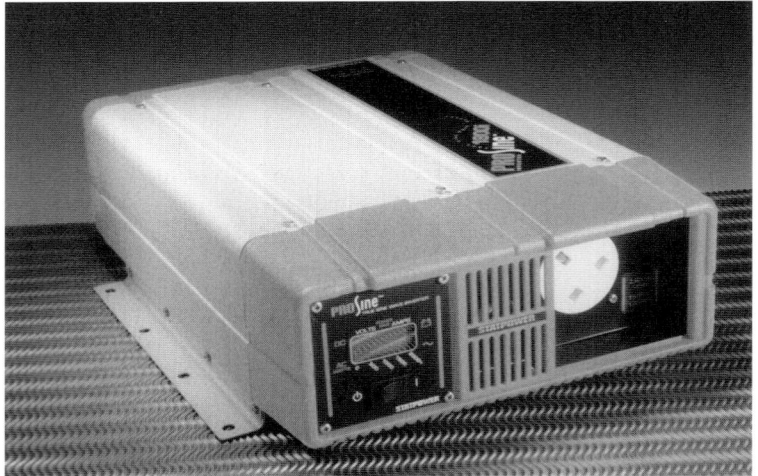

A more powerful unit will be required for desktop and marine PCs

If you have a well specified DC system on board, maybe with a separate 'navigation system' battery circuit, it is quite feasible to dispense with an inverter, to avoid the associated electrical losses. With desktop or marine PCs, it is usually possible to have the built-in 240VAC power supply unit replaced with a 12 or 24VDC unit.

Interference

One of the less welcome aspects of DC-AC power inverters can be electrical interference, which may interrupt radio reception and in some extreme cases cause problems with screen visibility. Produced as a by-product of the DC-AC conversion, waste energy is given off as heat (which is why larger inverters have 'heat sink' fins and must be sited correctly) as well as interference.

Coping with electrical interference on small boats can be a bit of a 'black art', but common remedies include: moving the inverter away from the PC, other electrics, instruments or wires that carry signals; orienting the inverter differently; fitting 'chokes' around video and signal cables.

The best way to avoid dealing with interference on board is to stop it happening in the first place. To this end, it is worth consulting a professional or asking a supplier for a trial unit before committing to a purchase. Generally though, most modern, pure sine-wave, hybrid units will produce acceptably small levels of electrical interference which can be dealt with by siting and installing the inverter sensibly.

Batteries and power generation

Whether running your PC through an inverter or direct from the boat's 12 or 24VDC supply, one thing is certain: you will wish you had bigger batteries!

It has been common practice for some years now for boats to have separate battery circuits for domestic power requirements and for engine starting. The obvious reason is that there should always be electrical power available to start the boat's engine, even if the domestic batteries are drained.

In a similar way, as yachtsmen become more and more reliant on electronics, there is a definite trend for on board electrical systems to become more powerful and more 'bullet-proof'. Indeed, it is not uncommon nowadays to see new boats equipped with three battery banks, intended for domestic power, engine start and, last but not least, critical navigation systems.

If you are planning to use your PC for navigation, especially chart plotting, or if you have many electronic navigation aids on board, you may consider fitting a separate battery and even a separate charging system, to ensure that these systems can be relied upon.

If you do fit extra battery capacity, you should also consider upgrading your charging capacity, maybe by fitting a bigger, or second, alternator, or a solar or wind charging system.

Uninterruptible power supplies (UPS)

You may consider fitting an uninterruptible power supply (UPS) to avoid your PC restarting if the electrical supply is interrupted or the voltage drops too low. If using an external UPS, it must be run off a 240VAC mains power supply (note if using an inverter it must be a true sine-wave inverter since other inverters will trip the UPS with each cycle, leaving it ticking like a clock as it trips in and out). Alternatively a UPS can be fitted inside a DC-powered marine PC, but the drawback with this is that it will only protect the processor unit and not the display in the event of a power outage.

Basic UPSs provide a fairly limited 'autonomy' from their internal batteries in the event of a power failure. This autonomy is intended to allow the PC to shut down 'gracefully' (by closing down programs in the correct sequence), not as an alternative means of operation. UPSs with significant autonomy (more than a couple of minutes) are not only very expensive, but also extremely heavy, being comprised of large, usually lead-acid, batteries.

Remote displays and workstations

Some users wish to display computer information remotely, or to operate the PC from a different part of the boat. Examples of this are having the chart plotter repeated to a screen up on deck, or having a PC shared between the saloon and the master cabin.

A video splitter can split the PC output to a number of repeater displays, at the same time boosting the signal strength to support longer cable runs. Alternatively a switch box can be used to equip some or all of these repeat stations with a keyboard and mouse, allowing full remote operation of the equipment.

There may also be a requirement to connect the PC together with an on board TV or video, to show computer output on the TV, or TV programmes on the PC monitor. Generally, these kinds of installation are best left to the professionals.

Anyone for television?

As television becomes more popular on small boats, finding space for both a computer display and TV screen can be challenging. When one considers that they are rarely used simultaneously, it can make sense to use the same screen for both purposes.

Outputting the PC display to a TV screen is relatively easy, with the video signal being provided by a TV converter (either an add-on, or built into the PC), and a modulator if necessary to change the TV channel used for the computer display. However, the resolution of a TV screen is much lower than a computer screen, so some loss of image quality may be experienced. Also, taking higher resolution PC output to a TV can be very expensive.

It is generally better to go the other route – fit a TFT flat screen PC monitor and convert the TV signal (PAL, NTSC or SECAM) to a computer signal. This can be done with a separate converter box, and the monitor can then be switched between TV and PC output as required.

Even better, with a marine PC, a TV expansion board can be fitted, which allows the TV image to be displayed in a window on the monitor or as a full screen image (as well as offering the facility to record video clips or still images for those so inclined). For the increasing number of PCs that are fitted with a DVD drive, you get the ability to play DVD films over the TV system as well – much more compact and reliable than video-cassettes. At present DVD players are designed to be locked into one of four world regions (they only play DVD discs from one region, to avoid customers buying cheaper videos from other regions); however, software tools are available to unlock the players and, in any case, multi-region DVD drives are becoming available.

Important Note – For those planning to travel greater distances, a word of caution is required concerning different TV and video signal formats. In the USA, TV signals conform to the NTSC standard, but this is not used in Europe where there are a number of versions of the PAL standard (PAL-I for the UK, and PAL B/G for most of southern Europe for example), and France uses its own SECAM format. Some TVs and videos will only work with the one format, while others will support either the range of PAL formats or NTSC, and a very few will support all formats.

Using a computer display connected to a PC with a TV expansion board would seem to be the route offering the widest range of options; however, this does mean that all TV viewing would have to be done through the PC.

Interfacing and NMEA0183 – the theory

Back in the early days of marine electronics, each piece of equipment was a stand-alone unit that could not communicate with the outside world. However, manufacturers quickly recognised that it would make sense if instruments could send and receive information to each other, and began designing instruments which could 'communicate'.

These new instrument systems were far more powerful than had been possible with stand-alone instruments – imagine how useful it is, for example, to be able to automatically work out the true wind speed and direction, given input from the log, compass and an apparent wind sensor.

This idea quickly caught on, but with the significant drawback that if a customer owned instruments from different manufacturers, it was extremely unlikely that these instruments would be able to 'talk' to each other. This is because each manufacturer used its own private or 'proprietary' communications language.

NMEA0183

In the early 1980s in the USA, the NMEA (National Marine Electronics Association) formed a communications standard intended to allow equipment from different manufacturers to communicate easily, with obvious benefits to the consumer.

The original standard went through a number of developments, but stabilised at the NMEA0183 standard. The result is that nowadays almost all instruments can send (and often receive) NMEA0183 data, even if manufacturers use their own proprietary communications system between their own instruments. Though the NMEA0183 specification is updated periodically to keep pace with new developments, it is 'backwardly-compatible' so newer equipment should always be able to send and receive NMEA0183 data that older compatible equipment can use.

At its most basic level, NMEA0183 communications consist of a 'talker' sending out data in 'sentences' to one or more 'listeners'. The talker does this regardless of whether or not a listener is connected, and in fact has no way of knowing if any other equipment is actually receiving the data.

This is an extremely powerful facility – NMEA0183 makes it possible to connect your PC to a wide variety of on board instruments and for software running on your PC to receive and use information the instruments transmit.

> **Tip** – Most people refer to the NMEA0183 specification as 'NEMA 183' which, although inaccurate, is phonetically far more convenient!

Electrical signals

It's important to note that NMEA0183 is not just a 'language', it actually consists of a full specification defining electrical signal levels as well as the format of the data to be used.

With NMEA0183 data is sent down a pair of wires, officially named A and B, but more usually called signal (+) and ground (–) or similar. A great deal of effort went into specifying a system that can travel long distances in an electrically noisy environment without becoming corrupted. The signal is 'differential' in that the logical status 'on' or 'off' is defined by the *difference* between the voltages on the signal and ground wires, rather than an absolute voltage. This means that electrical interference is minimised. Note that the voltage levels may be anything from 2V to 15V, well outside of the range in the PC's RS232 specification, though the use of a proper NMEA/RS232 converter will ensure that voltages are converted to and from the RS232 and NMEA0183 specifications.

Opto-isolation

As part of the NMEA specification, the listener device must be opto-isolated. At its simplest, this means that the incoming signal switches a bulb on and off, and the listener detects the state of the bulb. Just having on and off states for the bulb is another tool in the fight against interference, and the lack of a direct physical connection also minimises the risk of damage from voltage surges down the line.

Data format

NMEA0183 data can consist of a wide range of sentences, each with their own meaning, most of which are part of the specification and all use a common format.

Each sentence begins with a $ sign, then the next two characters identify the type of equipment sending the data. Next, three letters define the type of data that is held in the rest of the sentence. After this comes the data itself, with each item separated by a comma. At the end there may be an * followed by two characters. This is an

```
$GPRMC,153334,A,5051.64,N,00117.70,W,005.0,131.5,100295,004.3,W*7D
$GPRMB,A,0.00,L,,NAB,5040.05,N,00057.07,W,017.5,131.5,005.0,V*68
$GPR00,NAB,,,,,,,,,,,,,*08
$GPGLL,5051.64,N,00117.70,W*7A
$PGRMZ,-212,f,3*37
$GPXTE,A,A,0.00,L,N*6E
$GPBWC,153335,5040.05,N,00057.07,W,131.5,T,135.8,M,017.5,N,NAB*55
$GPRMC,153336,A,5051.64,N,00117.70,W,005.0,131.5,100295,004.3,W*7F
$GPRMB,A,0.00,L,,NAB,5040.05,N,00057.07,W,017.5,131.5,005.0,V*68
$GPWPL,5040.05,N,00057.07,W,NAB*15
$GPGLL,5051.64,N,00117.70,W*7A
$PGRMZ,-212,f,3*37
$GPXTE,A,A,0.00,L,N*6E
$GPBWC,153337,5040.05,N,00057.07,W,131.5,T,135.8,M,017.5,N,NAB*57
$GPRMC,153338,A,5051.64,N,00117.70,W,005.0,131.5,100295,004.3,W*71
```

NMEA0183 sentences have a standard structure optional checksum, which the listener can use to check whether the sentence has been corrupted in its transmission. See the diagram above which shows typical NMEA0183 sentences.

There are also manufacturer's proprietary sentences that begin with $P and then the manufacturer's ID, which can hold anything the manufacturer decides. Equipment normally transmits data in a sequence, with each sentence being repeated every one or two seconds (though this may be much more frequent).

Generally, this is straightforward and works pretty well in most cases, but because the standard has developed on a fairly *ad-hoc* basis, there can be some problems:

◆ First, a listener can decide which sentences (and even which parts of the sentence) it will interpret (or listen out for). This means that two NMEA0183 devices may not communicate at all if the talker is not outputting anything the listener understands.

◆ Secondly, the talker can decide not only which sentences to output, but it can also decide not to fill in all of the data in a sentence, and just leave some of it blank (though there are a few sentences where it is mandatory for all fields to be completed).

◆ Finally, for common items such as vessel position and depth the talker generally has a wide choice of sentences from which it can choose, each outputting similar (but not identical) sets of information. Because of all of this, it is worth checking with manufacturers or suppliers whether or not pieces of equipment will talk to each other.

Whilst it is generally acknowledged that it is not perfect, the NMEA0183 format has allowed a wide variety of instruments to work together, and any problems have tended to affect instrument manufacturers and installers more than end users. However, as an increasing amount of electronics is used on boats the standard is showing its age, and will probably be replaced in the next few years with a new format, NMEA2000, based on the CAN bus used in vehicle electronics. See chapter 11 for details on NMEA2000.

NMEA0183 Troubleshooting

Usually, NMEA0183 interfacing is quite straightforward and is simply a matter of methodically following manufacturers' instructions. Sometimes, though, you may experience problems. If you do, the following may prove useful:

If you are having trouble receiving or just want to look at NMEA0183 data, one of the easiest ways is to use the *Hyperterminal* software included with Windows 95/98 (note that *Hyperterminal* seems to be less reliable under Windows 98 than 95 and may occasionally lock up).

1   Confirm that the NMEA0183 device is switched on and set up to transmit data, by referring to its installation or user guide (some hand-held GPS sets won't export unless connected to an external 12VDC supply, using the manufacturer-supplied cable).

2   Set *Hyperterminal* up (serial port number usually COM1 or COM2, data rate 4800 bps, 8 data bits, 1 stop bit, no parity and no flow control), and when you connect the instrument(s) to the serial port you chose, you should see the NMEA0183 data streaming in. This input can be saved to disk or printed off, which can help manufacturers diagnose NMEA0183 incompatibilities.

If nothing appears in the *Hyperterminal* screen, you can use a voltmeter (set to DC Volts) across the A and B lines from the NMEA0183 device, and you should see the voltage fluctuate up and down as data passes down the line. If you see nothing, suspect a faulty or badly wired cable and double check that the GPS is set up to export data. Sometimes swapping the A and B lines over may solve problems.

Splitting and combining NMEA0183 signals

Because NMEA0183 data is just sent out regardless by the talker, its output can be split to a number of listeners. In many cases you can just divide the wires at a junction box, but sooner or later the electrical load imposed by each listener on the talker becomes too much, and the data breaks down into rubbish. If this happens, you need to go through a proper *distribution box* or *booster* that will increase the driver current available. The load of each listener, and the current available at each talker, can vary significantly, and there is no certain way of telling in advance whether a distribution box/ booster will be required.

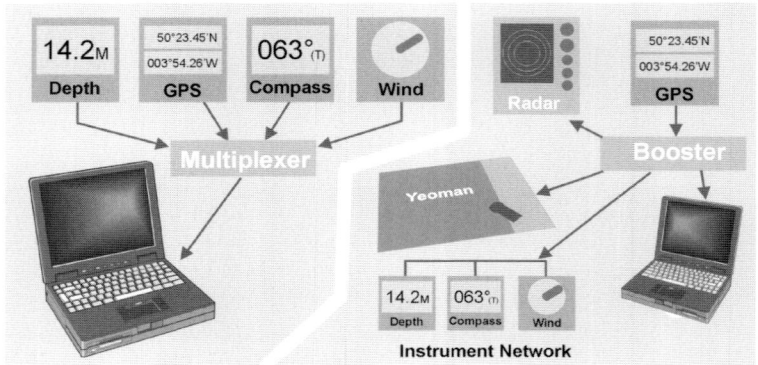

NMEA0183 signals may be easily split, combined and boosted for more complex installations

Sooner or later you will encounter the reverse problem – you want to combine data from a number of talkers into a device which may have just one listener port. For this you need a *multiplexer*, which is fitted with a number of listeners (usually four) and one talker. Incoming data on each listener port is held until a complete sentence is received and is then transmitted on the talker port. If the four inputs are all busy then their total input may well exceed the capacity of the talker, and some sentences may be dropped periodically. However, as almost all data is transmitted on a regular basis by the instruments, this seldom causes a problem.

If you need to multiplex more than four signals together it is possible to 'daisy-chain' NMEA0183 multiplexers together – ie connecting the output of a four-input multiplexer into one of the inputs of another similar multiplexer, thus obtaining seven inputs. If you plan to do this, please heed the advice above concerning exceeding the capacity of the talkers. Some multiplexers will get around this by setting the talker port up to transmit data at 9600 baud (twice as fast as standard NMEA0183), but make sure that the PC program you are using can receive NMEA0183 data at 9600 baud.

11 • Where Do We Go From Here?

History combined with a smattering of science provides a sound basis for predicting the future, though experience reminds us that both Mother Nature and the free market often confound those who dare to make predictions.

With this in mind, the reader should regard this section as being, at most, an educated guess. If our predictions prove to be even a little more accurate than the average weather forecast, we consider we have done our job well.

Backwards compatibility

When compared to other technical fields, marine electronics has progressed relatively slowly. However, we expect that the frenetic pace of development within computing and communications will transfer to the marine electronics world as the technologies move closer together.

This is exciting, because it should produce many more useful and innovative products for the mariner, and increasingly rapidly. The downside, of course, is the danger of obsolescence – many remember the VHS/Betamax dilemma in the 1980s.

The authors foresee that this should become less of a problem in marine computing. This is because manufacturers have learned that when they develop new technologies and standards, these should be designed to be backwardly compatible – that is, they should work with existing systems.

Backward compatibility is very important to customers because it lets them benefit from new technologies without having to completely replace existing equipment. This in turn benefits the manufacturers, because their customers are more likely to 'buy in' to the new technologies and to carry on purchasing shiny new pieces of kit for their boats.

However, not all manufacturers have seen the light, so before getting too excited when that new 'must have' product comes onto the market, do not assume that it will automatically work well with your existing systems – ask, ask, ask.

Instrument interfacing

Various versions of the NMEA0183 interface have been almost universal for some years now, but it has become increasingly stretched in terms of the amount of data it can carry; it is also not ideally suited to connecting many devices together. The National Marine Electronics Association (of America) is finalising details of a new protocol called NMEA2000, which is designed to overcome these limitations. NMEA2000 is designed to run on the CAN bus which was originally developed for the automotive industry – this allows equipment manufacturers to use standard and well-tried components which, due to economies of scale, are low in cost.

The new system is based on a single cable carrying both power and data to all components attached to it – they are simply 'teed off' where required. This gets around the problems of 'talkers' and 'listeners' which the NMEA0183 standard is based on, and saves having to run separate DC wires to some equipment. NMEA2000 will also be much faster than NMEA0183, achieved using a higher physical data rate and a very compact binary data format.

NMEA2000 has also allowed the designers to start with a clean sheet of paper and given them a chance to sort out redundancy and incompatibilities of data sentences which crept in as NMEA0183 developed over the years.

There will of course be drawbacks – for large yachts and commercial vessels the maximum length of the system (which is governed by signal timing requirements) could be a problem. But these kinds of potential problems can be overcome by the use of junction boxes (similar to 'routers' in a normal PC network).

Where a larger yacht has several PCs on board that are connected together with a normal computer network (Ethernet etc), it is possible to interface instruments directly onto the network using a network interface box. This makes NMEA data available to any PC on the network and can make installation much easier by minimising cable runs. A small network interface box plugs into the network in exactly the same way as a PC would, and may have four ports on it to accept up to four NMEA interfaces – of course, any number of these can be installed as required.

Other interfacing technologies are emerging which may suit the commercial marine world, but, designed for military uses, these are likely to be too expensive for widespread leisure marine use.

Computer hardware

Newly released computer processors usually double in perform-ance every couple of years, and certainly today's entry level processors are powerful enough to handle a boat's computing needs. Often, though, it is other parts of a PC that cause bottle-necks, especially in marine computing terms, where the PC needs to work with data from a number of sources.

Historically, getting data into and out of a PC has relied on passing the data through a limited number of serial ports, and it's true to say that serial port performance has not really kept up with proces-sor development. To get around this, a number of organisations have designed devices that offer different and faster routes from the outside world into and out of the PC.

One such device is the PC Card (which used to be called a PCMCIA card) which is now almost universal on laptop PCs. The PC Card allows a range of peripheral equipment (such as modems, hard disks, extra serial ports etc) to be easily connected to and recog-nised by the PC. Although PC Card technology initially looked quite promising, there have been problems with reliability and interfac-ing and very few desktop-type PCs have a PC Card reader fitted, so it is unlikely to become a universal standard.

More recently, the Universal Serial Bus (USB) looks to be able to deliver most of the benefits of PC Cards, but on all PCs. Most com-puters shipped today, whether desktops or laptops, are equipped with USB, and since the technology allows many peripherals to be 'daisy-chained' together using just one port on the PC, USB should be particularly useful in the marine computing world. Though ini-tially manufacturers were slow in creating peripherals that use USB, there are now many different devices (scanners, digital cameras, modems, printers etc) available.

The very first PCs were equipped with the internal ISA bus, which allows peripherals to be connected directly to it, using an 'expan-sion card'. Astonishingly, modern PCs still use this old and slow technology, although ISA does finally look to be on the way out and has to a large extent been replaced by the more modern PCI bus. This is powerful and fast and there are many peripherals avail-able whose expansion cards work with PCI. Therefore, this should continue to be an important and very common bus on PCs in spite of current limitations on the maximum number of PCI expansion cards that may be installed in one PC.

Of course it is possible that, for marine use, the architecture employed will become so specialised that in four or five years' time it may be hard to describe them as PCs in the accepted sense at all. Microsoft has been working on a cut-down version of Windows, called Windows CE, that is designed to run on small portable PCs. Windows CE is now quite established and marine software manufacturers are beginning to produce programs that work with CE.

If Windows CE-based PCs dispense with a number of PC-specific features and incorporate others as integrated components, it is quite feasible that they can be manufactured in volume at a lower price than a full PC. The question then is whether or not the market would be willing to accept a machine with this reduced functionality and whether a two-tier market for computing on board will develop.

Displays

Monitors, displays or screens. Call them what you will, but the majority available today are aimed at indoor, artificially lit, office or home environments. Laptop PCs have for some time been equipped with thin film technology (TFT) based liquid crystal displays (LCD) almost as standard, and whilst these have become available as separate units (again aimed at the office environment), they have really failed to deliver in the marine world.

Very few TFTs or traditional cathode ray tubes (CRTs) are designed to be waterproof or even water resistant. Those that are have tended to be very expensive. Lack of waterproofing may be less of a problem in a larger yacht with a relatively 'dry' navigation area.

It could be said that the weakness which has really held up the use of PCs on board is that of display brightness – anyone who has tried to use a cash dispenser in direct sunlight will appreciate that computer screens can be very difficult indeed to view outdoors.

While TFT displays are desirable because they are more compact and use much less electrical power than CRTs, the problem has always been with delivering sufficient brightness and contrast for the display to be useful in a range of lighting conditions.

The situation is now changing very rapidly, and while the holy grail of waterproof, bright, clear, high resolution colour displays at a low price has not yet been reached, two technologies are emerging which look very promising. First, super high brightness TFT displays, where a very powerful backlight gives a display that is bright enough to be read in direct sunlight. Secondly, we are now seeing the emergence of a number of transflective or reflective colour displays. These effectively have a mirror mounted behind the display, so the stronger the light on the display, the brighter it becomes. Although more promising in the longer term, the transflective displays at present suffer from low resolution, and are currently not very useful at night, but no doubt these issues will be overcome fairly soon.

The other major flat screen technology in the market is the plasma display. In manufacture, it is easy to make these very large, and so they are used for 40" and 60" TV or computer displays. Until now their resolution has been fairly low, at about 640x480, which has made them more suited for TV use or as presentation monitors viewed from a distance, but we are now seeing higher resolution models coming out specifically for the PC market.

Navigation

The main developments are expected to be in electronic charts and how they are used. Although raster chart formats such as ARCS and Maptech are quick and easy to produce, they are not as versatile as vector charts. Much is made in some circles of the forthcoming official S-57 edition 3 vector charts (ENCs) for the commercial market, but it is likely that their cost will be too high for most leisure users. Instead, we expect the existing publishers of vector charts, such as Euronav (Livechart), C-Map, Transas and Navionics, to extend their use in the leisure sector; indeed, there are very likely to be more competing formats arriving on the market in the next year or so.

That is not to say that there is little future for raster charts – far from it in fact. In the leisure market, in particular, the demand for plentiful, low cost chart coverage is set to be fulfilled by raster charts for some years to come.

We have seen that current leisure electronic charting systems offer facilities like tidal route planning and radar image overlay, but these (very powerful) features are generally passive. As the quality of available data increases, we expect to see more active and intelligent features emerging for leisure users. These will almost certainly include 3-dimensional underwater views; maybe the 'rolling road' seen on GPS units, but with chart information included. 'Head up' chart display as opposed to 'North up' will certainly become more common. Another area where we will see development is in passage planning: the navigation system could warn you if your passage plan or actual route takes you into dangerous waters or restricted areas. Examples might be cutting the corner off a headland or into a tidal race, or taking the wrong path through a traffic separation scheme. We also expect more intelligence in routeing; a system might give powerboats the best course and speed to make for a given ETA, or it might build up performance models of a sailing boat and calculate the best route taking into account wind and tide.

The aforementioned are not wholly in the category of 'crystal ball gazing'; many of these features are already included in some of the latest custom systems, but are not yet fully developed for standard off the shelf products. One thing is sure: although electronic charting programs have come a long way, there is plenty of scope for development into much more useful and powerful systems.

Weather information

Historically, all mariners have enjoyed access to free weather information, whether spoken forecasts and status reports received via consumer broadcast channels or full meteorological charts and other weather data obtained by listening in to radio transmissions between meteorological offices.

This situation is changing as European meteorological offices are driven to be increasingly commercial by their governments. Many regard this as a ludicrous situation, arguing that taxpayers have already paid once for collection and analysis and are expected to pay again to receive full weather information. Of more concern is the danger that leisure mariners might be less inclined to purchase adequate weather information and so put themselves and others at greater risk when they venture to sea.

With the exception of spoken weather information from the coastguard/broadcast media and text-only NAVTEX broadcasts as part of the GMDSS, in the UK at least, leisure sailors will need to pay for more and more weather information.

Unfortunately, this situation is unlikely to reverse in the near future and there will almost certainly be a development in the market for commercial weather services, whether run by meteorological offices or private organisations. Because of the need to control access to this commercial data, it will most likely be made available through premium rate phone or fax numbers, or as encrypted data via secure sites on the Internet or dedicated information servers. This commercialisation is already changing the way in which leisure sailors obtain weather information. Services that transmit weather information digitally so that it can be shown on top of an electronic chart will develop; we also expect to see greater provision of shore-based routeing services for longer passages and for racing yachts.

Communications

The growth of cellphones and other modern communications systems has had a massive impact on western society. Just look at how the cellphone has changed, and the whole nature of communications changed with it, over the past few years.

More recently, a whole new generation of satellite communications systems is becoming live, some of which compete against INMARSAT (though at time of writing none currently have INMARSAT's GMDSS capabilities).

At the same time long established communications services such as radio link calls over VHF, MF and HF are being closed down – this is because their use has petered out to an extent where these services are no longer commercially viable.

Satellite communications therefore will undoubtedly continue to improve and offer more and more to users, whether they are mariners or land-based.

Hidden behind the brave new world hype, though, are some important commercial facts: many of the satellite systems (intended mainly for land use) were planned several years ago, before GSM effectively became an international standard for cellphones. Many of the land-based *potential* customers of satellite systems have since found that their needs are completely met with cellphones. The combination of this smaller-than-expected subscription base for satellite communications, scattered over the oceans and on remote parts of the land, means that cost for users is bound to be higher than was initially forecast and will certainly remain significantly higher than for cellphones.

It's important to realise that receiving and transmitting data at a high data rate, for example browsing the WWW, will always be a problem with low cost satellite services aimed at leisure users. Newly emerging technology in cellphones means we may see the data rate quadrupling in a few years, but this will be of limited use for many yachtsmen because cellular radio technology is limited by range from the coast.

Satellite services need a directional dish to receive data at any but the slowest of data rates – whilst you can easily bolt a satellite dish to the side of your house, it is a lot more difficult and expensive to have a 1 metre stabilised dish on your boat! What this is likely to mean is that for the average leisure yachtsman, satellite data services will not be affordable or available through the WWW, but rather through access to dedicated data services that can send the required data somewhat more compactly and cheaply.

The early years of the twenty-first century will see a number of seamless dual technology devices appearing. These will take advantage of higher bandwidth cellular services when available; and will automatically drop back to slower (and more expensive) satellite communications, offering a reduced set of services when out of cell range.

In spite of these bandwidth limitations, an increasing number of yachtsmen will see basic e-mail and other data services as commonplace. This may be for simple communication with friends, family and office, or it may be for commercially run services such as updating a boat's charts with the latest corrections, obtaining new charts, or getting the latest weather forecast data. This capability is likely to be built into a PC-based marine software program – so that, for example, it may obtain the latest weather forecasts, NAVTEX messages and weather satellite images every six hours from a shore-based information source, automatically and totally transparently to you.

Systems monitoring and control

At present the main application areas for PCs on all but the biggest of boats are in navigation, communications and weather. However, as more powerful marine PCs are used, with improved interfacing capabilities, we will see them being used more for monitoring and control applications.

Monitoring and control programs let the yachtsman or a service engineer see trends of factors such as oil pressure, temperature etc. This information can highlight warning signs of equipment failure, or can be used for problem diagnosis. Such a program may also be linked to a service and maintenance program, so that the yachtsman is reminded of scheduled service intervals or any non-standard maintenance requirements.

Documentation

Buy a new boat in Europe these days and you will certainly receive many files containing the boatbuilder's and system manufacturers' own documentation, each in its own format and layout. Finding specific information when required, for example in the event of gear failure, can be a frustrating business. Also, most publications are vulnerable to damp and damage and may take up large amounts of stowage. Often, yacht owners will keep these important documents ashore and hope they never need them at sea.

In the near future, when most yachts will be supplied complete with a PC, it's likely that all this information will be put onto a CD-ROM or a DVD by the boatbuilder. This will give the yachtsman documentation that is virtually indestructible, takes up very little space, and can easily be accessed.

Taking things one step further, all relevant items could be indexed and cross referenced, so for example you could list equipment by location or by function, and use built-in links from, say, the engine documentation to its installation drawings.

Computer-ready boats

As more and more yachtsmen use PCs, many boatyards are starting to take notice and are providing suitable instrument interfaces for the owner to plug their laptop into. Some of the prestige boat manufacturers already offer complete PC packages on the boat's option list. This will become almost universal in the next few years as marine PCs become more prevalent and displays improve. As well as being driven by demand from customers, boatbuilders realise that this service can also save them money – fewer instrument displays are required, which saves costs on the equipment and also cable installation and joinery work.

Appendix 1 • Other Types of Personal Computer

Since the vast majority of computers used aboard boats conform to the definition in chapter 1, this book has focused on them. However, just so you don't miss out, and because one of the following may be more suitable for your needs, here is a brief description of other computers you might consider using:

Programmable calculators

These were the first type of computer used aboard leisure boats. They offered the navigator a small device capable of calculating simple mathematical functions. Since they didn't have much memory for storing data, the user would have to type in the required data and the calculator would run a small built-in sequence of mathematical operations on the data, presenting a numerical output which the user would then use in the traditional navigation process. Some models require the user to type in the 'programs' as well, having no way of storing this information when the unit is switched off.

Whilst programmable calculators are necessarily limited in their use, various manufacturers have enhanced the programs running on them and they can now store more 'user data'. They offer the benefits of relatively low cost, small size and low power consumption and are suited to the maths involved in astro navigation, thus they are quite common amongst blue-water sailors.

There are also some programmable calculators offering simple tidal calculations and even those that have a sufficiently large screen to draw a tidal curve in a graphical format.

Although programmable computers are not waterproof, water resistant pouches to protect them are available.

Palmtop computers

These small computers are much more powerful than programmable calculators and, as well as the built-in programs, you can buy or type in a range of programs to extend their use.

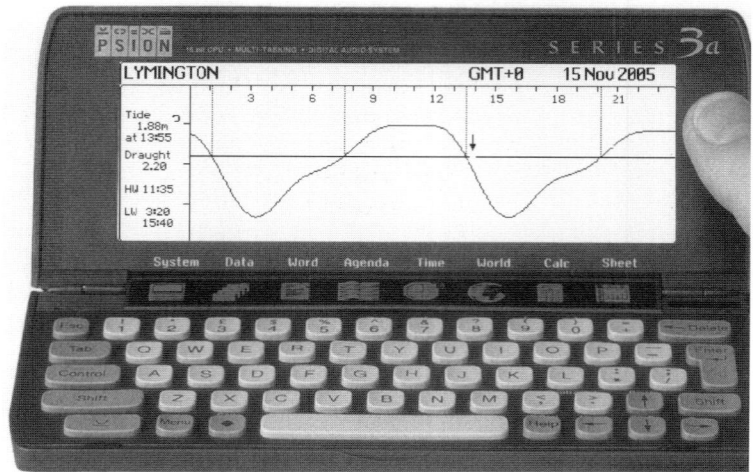

Limited by small screens, palmtop computers can nevertheless be very useful on board

Palmtops are a 'halfway house' between programmable calculators and PCs – relatively inexpensive, very small, and again using little power. They can do a lot more than the calculators, but smaller models can be limited in their use on board because they don't really have big enough screens to display charts or other graphical information conveniently.

Three of the more popular brands available are some of the Windows CE machines, such as the Hewlett-Packard Journada; others include the Palm Pilot and the Psion 3 and 5 ranges.

It's worth bearing in mind that because these are 'proprietary' computer designs, they will usually only run programs written specially for them. Currently, a program written for one Windows CE palmtop will not necessarily run properly, if at all on another CE model. Although this situation is likely to change in the near future, potential buyers should be aware of this limitation.

As palmtops have developed over the last few years, they have tended to become larger and more like normal laptop computers, at the same time as laptops are getting smaller. This trend is likely to continue until it will be very hard to tell them apart!

Again, palmtops are not usually waterproof, although there are waterproof cases available to fit them.

The Apple Macintosh

The 'Mac', like the PC, is also a 'real computer', capable of doing everything you are likely to want to do with a PC on board. Indeed it is often argued in the computer press that Macs are better designed and easier to use than PCs. Both 'camps' have strong followings and users have been known to get very animated over why their favourite is 'best'.

The reality is that whilst it is hard to say that either type is better or worse than the other, market activity over the last few years has resulted in there being an awful lot more PCs on desks than Macs.

So what does this mean for yachtsmen? Ultimately if you own a PC, there will be a far greater choice of programs to choose from than those written specifically for Macs.

This does not mean that Macintosh users have no choices at all; there are some excellent marine programs that have been written for the Mac and an owner may also be able to run PC software on their Mac through the use of an 'emulator' program (see below).

If a Macintosh owner can't find suitable marine software written for their Mac, it's worth pointing out that PCs are now so inexpensive that Mac owners have been known to purchase a laptop PC simply to gain access to the marine software system of their choice.

PC emulators for the Macintosh

Some Macintosh users may run PC marine software on their Macs using a PC emulator program. There are some *caveats* with emulators, though: firstly, the emulator uses machine resources when running – your Mac may not have enough memory left to run its own operating system, the emulator program, Windows and the PC program at the same time. Also it quite simply may not be fast enough to work at an acceptable speed. Secondly, some PC programs require a dongle to be plugged into the PC's printer ('parallel') port, and Macs do not normally have this type of port fitted. Lastly, many marine programs use the PC's serial port to read data from the GPS; and whilst Macs have serial ports, connectors may differ or there may be compatibility problems.

There is no easy way to tell if an emulator will allow you to use a particular PC marine program on your Mac. The author's advice is to actually see the program (or at least a demonstration version) running on a Mac/emulator combination before parting with your money – since PC software is not intended to work on Macs, there may be a re-stocking fee if you return a system for this reason.

The authors make no apologies for the fact that the following is not an exhaustive list of all possible suppliers.

The companies we have chosen for inclusion have been selected because, either as manufacturers or dealers, they have been active in this field for some time and are therefore probably the best equipped to give you good advice and service.

Manufacturer or dealer?

It may be thought that it is best to go direct to the manufacturers for some items, maybe in the hope of obtaining better pricing. This is often not the case: remember that they specialise in manufacturing, not end-user support, and that you may have to pay for technical support from the manufacturer whereas a dealer may include this as part of their service – always ask!

Specialist marine hardware and software dealers get good pricing from the manufacturers which enables them to be very competitive on price. When you also consider that they are experienced in installing, integrating and configuring a whole range of marine PC systems, they are much better placed than some manufacturers to provide a complete service and to offer good, unbiased advice.

As a final word, if you are planning to purchase anything to do with PCs, it is wise to contact as many suppliers as possible, and not just to confine yourself to the companies listed.

Computer manufacturers

Because of the large amount of computer brands currently available, it is impracticable to list them all here. Instead, the reader who is looking to buy a laptop or a desktop PC directly by mail order is advised to consult one of the many mainstream PC magazines. If you do not feel sufficiently knowledgeable to make this decision yourself, it is well worth contacting an experienced marine computing specialist who, for a small price premium, will be able to supply a PC that is suitable for your needs.

Such a specialist will also be aware of more rugged marinised units designed for use on board and which may not be widely advertised. The cost of these units is falling all the time and the market is changing rapidly, so ask lots of questions to make sure you are getting good advice.

Finally, though, as well as contacting the companies listed below, don't forget to try your usual chandlery – a few now have dedicated PCs and trained staff to demonstrate software products; and you, the customer, can encourage them by asking for these products.

All sources shown have been checked and were correct at time of going to press.

ARCS – See United Kingdom Hydrographic Office

Bonito
Gerichtsweg 3   Tel: +49 5052 6052
D-29320 Hermansburg   Fax: +49 5052 3477
Germany   www.bonito.net

* Board Terminal – weatherfax/radio software
* Pro Meteo – weatherfax software

BSB – See Nautical Data Ltd

Burmarc Ltd
Unit 12   Tel: 01428 724777
Beaver Industrial Estate   Fax: 01428 724652
Liphook   www.burmarc.co.uk
GU30 7EU

* Winchart – chart plotting software
* Pocket Winchart – chart plotting for Hewlett Packard CE machines

C-Map UK Ltd
Systems House   Tel: 01329 517777
Delta Business Park   Fax: 01329 517778
Salterns Lane   www.c-map.com
Fareham   PO16 0QS

* C-Map electronic cartography (vector)

Chartwork Ltd – See Burmarc Ltd

Dartcom
Powdermills   Tel: 01822 880253
Postbridge   Fax: 01822 880232
Yelverton   www.dartcom.co.uk
Devon PL20 6SP

* Winsat – weather satellite software

Dolphin Maritime Software Ltd
713 Cameron House   Tel: 01524 841946
White Cross   Fax: 01524 841946
South Road
Lancaster LA1 4XQ

* Marine software products for hand-held computers and PCs

Euronav Ltd
20 The Slipway   Tel: 02392 373855
Port Solent   Fax: 02392 325800
Portsmouth PO6 4TR   www.euronav.co.uk

* seaPro 2000 – chart plotting system

Garmin (Europe) Ltd
Unit 5, The Quadrangle   Tel: 01794 519944
Abbey Park Industrial Estate   Fax: 01794 519222
Romsey   www.garmin.com
Hampshire   SO51 9AQ

* GPS equipment

Global Navigation Software Co
5026 West Point Loma Blvd   Tel: +1 619 225 0792
San Diego
California 92107
USA

* NavPak chart plotting system

Globe Wireless
Admiraal de Ruyterstraat 20   Tel: +31 (0) 10 426 09 70
3115 HB Schiedam   Fax: +31 (0) 10 426 09 51
The Netherlands   www.globewireless.com

* HF radio communication and e-mail

Icom (UK) Ltd
Sea Street   Tel: 01227 741741
Herne Bay   Fax: 01227 741742
Kent CT6 8LD   www.icomuk.co.uk

* Conventional and PC controlled radio receivers and transceivers

ICS Electronics Ltd
Unit V   Tel: 01903 731101
Rudford Industrial Estate   Fax: 01903 731105
Ford   www.icselectronics.co.uk
Arundel
West Sussex BN18 0BD

* Fax III – weatherfax software
* WS5 – weather satellite system

Information Management Consultants
Media House   Tel: 0151 236 4124
Mann Island   Fax: 0151 236 9907
Liverpool L3 1DQ   www.super-hub.com

* Super-hub wireless data communications

Informatique et Mer
Technopole Izarbal   Tel: +33 559 43 81 00
F-64210 Bidart   Fax: +33 559 43 81 01
France   www.maxsea.com

* Maxsea – chart plotting software
* Macsea – chart plotting software for Macintosh
* Mapmedia – electronic charts (raster)

Jeppesen Marine
27350 SW95th Ave, Ste 3018
Wilsonville   Tel: +1 503 404 2700
OR 97070   Fax: +1 503 404 2701
USA   www.jeppesenmarine.com

* Electronic charting system

Kelvin Hughes
Kilgraston House   Tel: 023 8063 4911
Southampton Street   Fax: 023 8033 0014
Southampton   www.kh-online.co.uk
SO15 2ED

* Electronic charts and chart plotting software

Klas Ltd
Bracetown Business Park   Tel: +353 1 6624270
Clonee   Fax: +353 1 6624272
Co. Meath   www.klasisdn.com
Republic of Ireland

* PC interface cards for satellite communications

Lightmaster Software
166 Godstone Road   Tel: 0181 660 8451
Purley   Fax: 0181 660 6743
Surrey CR8 2DF   www.lightmaster.co.uk

* Lightmaster range of training and simulation software

Livechart – see Euronav Ltd

Magellan – see Next O'Gara

Mapmedia – See Informatique et Mer

Maptech Inc (UK Distributor:
Nautical Data Ltd)
1 Riverside Drive   Tel: +1 888 839 5551
Andover   Fax: +1 978 933 3040
MA 01810-1122   www.maptech.com
USA

**Marine Computing
International Ltd** (ex TT Designs)
Hamble Court   Tel: 02380 458047
Verdon Avenue   Fax: 02380 458057
Hamble   www.marinecomputing.com
SO31 4HX

* Complete range of marine software products
* Marine PCs and displays
* Installation, configuration and training

Maritek
1-D7 Templeton Centre   Tel: 0141 554 2492
Glasgow   Fax: 0141 639 1910
G40 1DA   www.maritek.co.uk

* Tidal software for Psion hand-held computers
* Bosun – vessel management for Psion

Mastervolt UK Ltd
Unit D5, The Premier Centre   Tel: 01794 516443
Abbey Park Industrial Estate Fax: 01794 516453
Romsey   SO51 9AQ   www.mastervolt.co.uk

* Inverters and battery chargers

Meridian Chartware Ltd
50 Unthank Road   Tel: 01603 441026
Norwich   Fax: 01603 765253
NR2 2RF   www.dspace.dial.pipex.com/meridian/

* SEAtrak RCDS – chart plotting software

Merlin Equipment
Unit 1 Hithercroft Court   Tel: 01491 824333
Lupton Road   Fax: 01491 824466
Wallingford
OX10 9BT

* Inverters, AC and DC electrical generation and storage

Nautical Data Ltd   Tel: 01243 377977
12 North Street   Fax: 01243 379136
Emsworth PO10 7DQ   www.nauticaldata.com

* Seafile Electronic – electronic almanac
* Maptech/BSB – electronic charts (raster)
* Maptech chart plotting software

Nautical Software – See Nobeltec

Nautical Technologies Ltd
217 Burleigh Road   Tel: +1 207 942 4751
Bangor   Fax: +1 207 941 1672
Maine 04401   www.thecapn.com
USA

* EasyNav – chart plotting software
* The Cap'n – chart plotting software

Navionics UK
PO Box 38   Tel: 01752 482632
Plymouth   Fax: 01752 481047
PL9 8YY   www.navionics.com

* Navionics electronic cartography (vector)

Neptune Navigation Software
PO Box 5106   Tel: 0118 988 5309
Riseley   Fax: 0870 0567329
RG7 1FD   www.neptunenav.demon.co.uk

* Neptune – tidal software
* Neptune – chart plotting software

Next O'Gara
25 The Clarendon Centre   Tel: 01722 410800
Salisbury Business Park   Fax: 01722 410777
Salisbury   www.next-destination.co.uk
Wiltshire SP1 2TJ

* Magellan GPS distributors
* Mini-M Satellite phones

Nobeltec
14657 SW Teal Blvd., Suite 132
Beaverton   Tel: +1 503 579 1414
Oregon 97007   Fax: +1 503 579 1304
USA   www.nobeltec.com

* Visual Series – chart plotting software
* Chartview – chart plotting software
* Tides & Currents – tidal software
* Radar PC (Koden & Nobeltec)

Northport Systems Inc.
73 Warren Road   Tel: +1 416 920 0447
Toronto   Fax: +1 416 964 6313
Ontario   www.fugawi.com
Canada M4V 2R9

* Fugawi – chart plotting system

PC Maritime Ltd
Bain Clarkson House
Brunswick Road
Plymouth
PL4 0NP

Tel: 01752 254205
Fax: 01752 253599
www.pcmaritime.co.uk

* Navmaster – chart plotting software
* PC Weatherfax for Windows
* NavTides
* Various simulators, tutorials and games

PC Plotter
The Boathouse
Brook Close
Sandown
IoW PO36 9PY

Tel/Fax: 01983 408951

www.pcplotter.freeserve.co.uk

* PC Plotter – chart plotting software

PinOak Digital
PO Box 360
Gladstone
NJ 07934-0360
USA

Tel: +1 908 234 2020
Fax: +1 908 234 9685
www.pinoak.com

* HF radio communication and e-mail

Pinpoint Systems International
381-4 Old Riverhead Road
Westhampton Beach
New York 11978
USA

Tel: +1 516 288 0264
Fax: +1 516 288 0294
www.pinpointsys.com

* Softchart & NOS/GEO electronic cartography (raster)

Quintessence Designs
PO Box 228
Emporium
Pennsylvania 15834
USA

Tel: +1 215 698 2424
Fax: +1 978 383 6464
www.quintessencedesigns.com

* Range of marine software for the Macintosh

Raytheon Marine Company
Anchorage Park
Portsmouth
PO3 5TD

Tel: 02392 693611
Fax: 02392 694642
www.raymarine.com

* Raytech – chart plotting software

SCS Mare
Via Gandhi 29   Tel: +39 02 939 09430
20017 Mazzo di Rho   Fax: +39 02 939 09431
Milano   www.scsmare.com
Italy

* Logbook – chart plotting software

Servowatch Systems
Thalest House   Tel: 01245 360019
Hatfield Peverel   Fax: 01245 362129
Essex CM3 2EH   www.servowatch.co.uk

* Instrumentation logging and control systems for larger yachts

Softwave
Riverside   Tel: 01628 637777
Mill Lane   Fax: 01628 773030
Taplow   SL6 0AA   www.softwave.co.uk

* Marine PCs and displays
* Electronic charting products

Transas Marine Ltd
Commodore House   Tel: 02380 332730
Mountbatten Business Centre Fax: 02380 233439
16–18 Millbrook Road East www.transas.com
Southampton SO15 1HY

* Tsunamis – chart plotting software
* Transas/Passport – electronic charts (vector)

Trimble Navigation Europe Ltd
Meridian Office Park   Tel: 01256 760150
Osborn Way   Fax: 01256 760148
Hook RG27 9HX   www.trimble.com/sales/uk.htm

* GPS equipment

United Kingdom Hydrographic Office
1 Admiralty Way   Tel: 01823 337900
Taunton   Fax: 01823 323753
TA1 2DN   www.hydro.gov.uk

* ARCS raster charts

Victron Energie
Wheatfield Way   Tel: 01455 618666
Hinckley Fields   Fax: 01455 611446
Hinckley LE10 1YG   www.imv.co.uk

* Inverters and battery chargers

Glossary

Algorithm – A set of well-defined rules or operations designed to solve a particular problem reliably and efficiently

AM – Amplitude modulation. Where the carrier signal's amplitude (size) changes according to the frequency of an applied signal

ANSI – American National Standards Institute

ARCS – Admiralty raster chart service. Range of electronic raster versions of UKHO paper charts

ARPA – Automated radar plotting aid

ASCII – American Standard Code for Information Interchange. System whereby numbers, letters and symbols are expressed as numbers for easy processing by computers

Bandwidth – The amount of data that can be sent through a given communications system in a given period of time

Baud – Unit of signal frequency in signals per second. Not synonymous with bits per second because signals can represent more than one bit. Baud equals bits per second only when the signal represents a single bit

Binary – Characteristic of having only two states, such as on or off. The binary number system uses only ones and zeros

Bit – Binary digit. The basic unit of all digital communications. A bit is a 'one' or 'zero' in a binary language

BPS – Bits per second. A measure of transmission speed

Bus – Data interfacing system that joins PC components together

Byte – A data unit of eight bits

Carrier Signal – A continuous waveform (usually electrical) with properties capable of being modulated or impressed with a second information-carrying signal

CCITT – Committee Consultatif Internationale de Telegraphique et Telephonique. The International Telegraph and Telephone Consultative Committee, once part of the ITU

CD-ROM – Compact disc – read only memory

CRC – Cyclic redundancy check

CRT – Cathode ray tube. Traditional 'tube' used for TV or computer monitor display

CW – Carrier wave

DC – Direct current

DGPS – Differential GPS. A technique to improve GPS accuracy that uses pseudo-range errors recorded at a known location to improve the measurements made by other GPS receivers within the same general geographic area, with corrections transmitted over radio

Digital – The method of representing information as numbers with discrete (non continuous) values, usually expressed as a sequence of binary digits (ones and zeros)

DMA – Direct memory access or Defense Mapping Agency (US)

DoD – Department of Defense (US)

DRAM – Dynamic random access memory

Duplex – Characteristic of data transmission. Either full or half-duplex. Full permits simultaneous two-way communication. Half means only one side can talk at once

DVD – Digital versatile disk. A much higher capacity development of the CD-ROM, used for computer data storage and as a replacement for the video cassette

ECDIS – Electronic chart display and information system. A special term that refers to large ship bridge navigation systems conforming to standards laid down by the IMO

ECS – Electronic charting system. General term used to describe any computerised system capable of displaying electronic charts

EMC – Electromagnetic compatibility. The ability of electrical and electronic devices to work together without interference problems

ENC – Electronic navigational chart – A special term referring to electronic charts that conform to specific international standards for use with commercial ECDIS bridge systems

EPIRBs – Electronic Position Indicating Radio Beacons

ETSI – European Telecommunications Standards Institute. A counterpart to ANSI, facilitating integration of telecommunications standards into all of Europe and co-ordinating telecommunications policies

FAQ – Frequently asked questions.

FEC – Forward error correction. An error correction method used in data transmission

FM – Frequency modulation

FSK – Frequency shift keying modulation method

FTP – File transfer protocol. Internet service for up and downloading files efficiently

GMDSS – Global Maritime Distress and Safety System. A global standard for signalling and dealing with marine distress situations, using a combination of VHF, MF/HF radio, INMARSAT A, B and C and

GMT – Greenwich Mean Time

GPS – Global positioning system. A series of satellites combined with specialised devices that allow you to pinpoint exact locations anywhere on the earth, typically, Longitude and Latitude. A space-based radio positioning system which provides suitably equipped users with accurate position, velocity and time data. GPS provides this data free of direct user charge worldwide, continuously and under all weather conditions. The GPS constellation consists of 24 orbiting satellites, four equally spaced around each of six different orbital planes

GSM – Global System for Mobile Communications, or Groupe Spéciale Mobile. A pan-European cellular phone system that allows European travellers to use a single cellular phone in many different countries and have all calls billed to one account. Adopted as the preferred cellular standard in Europe, Asia and North America

HCRF – Hydrographic Chart Raster Format. The standard created by the UKHO for their ARCS raster charts, now being adopted by other hydrographic offices as well

HDOP – Horizontal dilution of precision. A measure of how much the geometry of the GPS satellites affects the position estimate (computed from the satellite range measurements) in the horizontal East/North plane

Hz – Hertz. Unit of frequency

IEEE – Institute of Electrical and Electronics Engineers. A worldwide engineering publishing and standards-making body for the electronics industry

IHO – International Hydrographic Organisation

IMO – International Maritime Organisation. Intergovernmental organisation with responsibility for maintaining standards of safety at sea

INMARSAT – International Maritime Satellite Organisation

ISA – Industry Standard Architecture bus. The original PC bus, still fitted to machines but largely superseded by the PCI bus.

ISDN – Integrated Services Digital Network. A high speed data line (64kbps) used as an alternative to a normal phone line, and also available over the INMARSAT B system

ISO – International Standards Organisation. Devoted to determining standards for international and national data communications

ISP – Internet service provider. A company that gives the public access to the internet

ITU – International Telecommunications Union. An organisation established by the United Nations and having as its membership virtually every government in the world

ITU-T – International Telecommunications Union Telecommunications. An international body of member countries whose task is to define recommendations and standards relating to the international telecommunications industry. Has replaced the CCITT as the world's leading telecommunications standards organisation

kbps – Kilobits per second. A measure of transmission speed

kHz – Kilohertz. One thousand Hertz, or cycles, per second

LES – Land earth station. This station is the interface between a communications satellite and the land based phone system

Lithium Ion (Li-Ion) battery – An efficient battery technology, supporting relatively long standby and talk time with no memory effect

LOA – Length over all

LSB – Lower side band

Mbps – Megabits per second. A million bits per second, a measure of transmission speed

MHz – Megahertz. One million Hertz, or cycles per second

Modem – A device that links computers via telephone lines and enables the transmission of data. The name comes from 'modulate' and 'demodulate': a modem converts (modulates) the PC's signals from digital to analogue for transmission over telephone lines. At the other end, another modem converts them back (demodulates) from analogue to digital

Modulation – Superimposing data on top of a 'carrier' signal such that when the carrier signal is removed, the original data is left

Motherboard – Part of the computer system that includes data pathways between each major system component

MS-DOS – Microsoft Disk Operating System. A text-based operating system, common in the 1980s and early 1990s. In fact, Microsoft Windows 95 and 98 both run on top of a special version of MS-DOS, but it is mostly hidden from the user

MTBF – Mean time between failure. The average time a device runs until it fails

NiCad – Nickel cadmium. A type of battery

NiMH – Nickel metal hydride. A type of battery

NMEA – National Marine Electronics Association (US)

NMEA0183 – A standard protocol deviced by the NMEA to enable instruments to communicate with each other (and also with computers)

NOAA – US National Oceanographic and Aeronautical Administration

Non-volatile (memory) see NVRAM

NVRAM – Non-volatile random access memory

OEM – Original equipment manufacturer

Opto-isolator – A device used to help eliminate electrical interference, and also to protect devices from electrical surges down data cables. It is required to be fitted on the receive side of all NMEA0183 interfaces.

Packet – A bundle of data, usually in binary form, organised in a specific way for transmission. Three principal elements are included in the packet: 1, control information such as destination, origin and length of packet; 2, the data to be transmitted; and 3, error-detection and correction bits

Parallel port – A port used for interfacing to printers and other devices. A number of data lines are used to send multiple items of data at once, as opposed to a serial port where the data just goes down one data line

PC Card (formerly PCMCIA card). Credit sized cards for use with laptop PCs, defined by the PCMCIA standard. The PCMCIA standards include three types, distinguished by increasing thickness: type 1: very thin memory cards, seldom used, type 2: most modems and interfaces; type 3: double thickness cards used for disk drives.

PCB – Printed circuit board

PCI – The standard bus for internal PC expansion cards, much faster than the ISA bus also installed in most machines.

PCMCIA – See PC Card

Protocol – A specific set of rules, procedures or conventions relating to format and timing of data transmission between two devices

Psion – A manufacturer of hand held computers, with their own proprietary operating system

PSTN – Public switched telephone network. Usually refers to the worldwide voice telephone network accessible to all those with telephones and access privileges. The PSTN is a gigantic maze of switching computers that can connect any two telephone points in potentially hundreds of different ways

RAM – Random access memory. Read-write volatile memory that is lost when power is discontinued; temporary storage

Raster – An image represented as a regular grid of different colour pixels. In charts, used to refer to scanned in charts

RS232 – The standard protocol used for serial ports on PCs

RS422 – A serial data standard used by Macintosh computers and also an element of the NMEA specification

SA – Selective availability. The method used by the DoD to control access to the full GPS accuracy

SCSI – Small computer systems interface. An interface used for high performance hard disks, CD-ROM drives and some other peripherals

SMS – Short message service. Enables a GSM phone to send a short text message to another GSM phone

SOLAS – Safety of life at sea

SSB – Single side band

Synchronous – Signals that are sourced from the same timing reference and have the same frequency; events that happen at the same time with respect to network timing

TCP/IP – Transmission Control Protocol/Internet Protocol. The network protocol used for the internet and for many local area computer networks

TFT – Thin film transistor. Technology used to produce flat panel computer and TV displays

UHF – Ultra high frequency

UKHO – United Kingdom Hydrographic Office

USB – Universal serial bus. A method of linking numerous external devices to a PC

USB – Upper side band

UTC – Universal Time Coordinated. This time system uses the second defined true angular rotation of the earth measured as if the earth rotated about its conventional terrestrial pole. However, UTC is adjusted only in increments of 1 second. The time zone of UTC is that of GMT

Vector – A line defined by its start point, direction and length. In terms of charts, vector charts refer to charts where the data is held in a database of points, lines, areas and symbols.

VHF – Very high frequency

Volatile (memory) – memory whose contents are lost when the power is switched off, for example the memory chips installed in PCs

WGS84 – World Geodetic System (1984). A mathematical ellipsoid designed to fit the shape of the entire earth. It is often used as a reference on a worldwide basis, while other ellipsoids are used locally to provide a better fit to the earth in a local region. GPS uses the centre of the WGS84 ellipsoid as the centre of its reference frame

Index

Free Demonstration CD-ROM Voucher

The authors have prepared a companion CD-ROM to this book. The CD-ROM contains free software, trial versions and demonstrations of a range of marine software.

If you would like to receive a copy of this CD-ROM, absolutely free of charge, complete this form and post it to:

> Using PCs on Board
> PO Box 41
> EMSWORTH
> PO10 8YL

If you have access to the Internet and prefer not to cut this voucher out of the book, simply complete the on-screen form at the following web address: http://www.pconboard.co.uk/democd.htm

Initials: _____   Surname: _____

Address: _____

_____

Town: _____   Postcode: _____

Country: _____

Daytime Telephone: _____

E-mail address: _____

Please complete the following questions:

Boat owner?   Y/N   If so, size LOA: _____ft/m

Manufacturer?   eg Moody, Beneteau, one-off _____

Sailing area? _____

Do you own a: Desktop PC? Y/N   Laptop PC? Y/N   Rugged PC? Y/N

Do you use a PC on your boat?   Y/N

Is it a ❏ laptop   or ❏ permanently fixed?

Age group?   13–21 ❏   22–34 ❏   35–44 ❏   45–54 ❏   55–64 ❏   65+ ❏